How Small a Whisper

How Small a Whisper

Evangelistic Messages and Outlines

Roger Carswell

Foreword by Warren W. Wiersbe

BAKER BOOK HOUSE
Grand Rapids, Michigan 49516

To
My father and mother
whose lives and example
made it so much easier
to seek and to keep
the fifth commandment

Contents

Foreword

Roger Carswell is a new name to Christians in America, but not to the church in Great Britain; for there he is rapidly being recognized as an effective young evangelist and Bible teacher.

Roger and I shared a conference at Torquay a few years ago; and from the first time I heard him preach, I was drawn to him. I heard in his messages an authentic note of true biblical evangelism, and I sensed in his spirit a sincere burden for lost souls.

His messages are biblical but not "preachy," and contemporary but not "trendy." They are interesting and yet convicting! Best of all, his messages are backed up by a life of discipline and devotion that is real.

I encouraged Roger to publish some of his messages, and this book is the result. My prayer is that God will use these sermons to win the lost as well as to stir the church to serve our Lord with greater zeal and holiness.

Warren W. Wiersbe

Preface

Earth is suspended in space. The clouds carry rain. There is a rotation of light and darkness. The tidal power of the sea is immense. Storms are stirred and stilled. Yet, says Job, all these are a mere whisper to the truth of God (*see* Job 26).

God has revealed himself to mankind in five basic ways. First, through creation—the material word; second, through individual conscience—the unspoken word; third, through the Scripture—the written word; fourth, through Christ—the living and loving Word; and fifth, through Christian conversion—the experienced word.

A preacher's privileged duty is to herald not only the fact of God, but also his Gospel: *Christ Jesus came into the world to save sinners.*

Creation itself is described by Job as "the mere edges of His ways," and he could conclude: "how small a whisper we hear of Him" (26:14). Yet how meager by comparison are these twenty-one messages here put into print. However, I pray that my "small whisper" may be used by God to speak to the spiritually deaf and dead so that they might hear and live!

1

Have You Heard the Voice of God?

> The voice of the LORD is over the waters; The God of glory thunders . . . . The voice of the LORD is full of majesty (Ps. 29:3–4).

An old Spanish lady thanked God for the prospect of one month in solitary confinement, part of her five-year prison sentence for "not being able to stop speaking" about the Lord Jesus. "Now I can be alone with the Lord Jesus," she explained.

Christ's beloved disciple, John, must have experienced similar emotions. As a disciple he was the youngest, and now he had outlived the other eleven. He was, however, spending his last days imprisoned on the small island of Patmos in the Aegean Sea. On this small volcanic mountain, John would have grown accustomed to the noise of the breakers beating against the rocks. He was alone in his cell, yet he was not cast down. It was here that God revealed insights into what was to happen in the future, commanding John: "Write the things which you have seen, and the things which are, and the things which will take place after this" (Rev. 1:19). As John listened to the voice of God, he likened it to "the sound of many waters" (v. 15; cf. Ezek. 1:24; 43:2).

John was familiar with the sound of the sea and the voice of God. To him they were both idyllic music.

How beautiful is the sound of waters rippling, rolling, and roaring as they continue their course unaltered by the apathy, animosity, or even the admiration of humans. On the hillsides emerge streams that barely trickle over their course, but gradually they gather momentum as they mingle and merge with others into a melodious harmony moving toward the mighty, powerful sea.

God's voice was as "the sound of many waters" to John. In similar fashion, the variety of streamlets that comprise the voice of God combine to form an irresistible torrent that tells us many things. Have you ever taken time to listen to God? The voice is a:

A Creative Voice

In the beginning, God spoke to nothing and he created from it something. "By faith we understand that the worlds were framed by the word of God, so that the things which are seen were not made of things which are visible" (Heb. 11:3). To those who will hear, all creation speaks of the fact that there is a Creator. Seven times in Psalm 29 we read of "the voice of the LORD." The number seven often signified completeness in the Old Testament. Wherever there is a list of seven things in the Bible, the center one is the hub. In this psalm's symbolism, the voice of the Lord breaks "the cedars of Lebanon," which, of course, were used in building Solomon's temple. God's voice thus created and provided a way whereby his creation could worship him.

Man "creates" only by taking something already there and revising it. All labor outside the spiritual realm basically involves moving the world's resources from one place to another or making something different by combining them. In contrast, it is the pattern of God that he takes *nothing* and makes something brand-new out of it. He did that literally in creation, and has been doing so figuratively ever since. In that way God took a tinker and made him into the great author/preacher, John Bunyan, and transformed a mere cobbler into William Carey, the founder of English missions. When God spoke to Gladys Aylward, an uneducated chambermaid, she became a great missionary to China. The voice of the Lord is a creative force.

A Commanding Voice

As the Creator, the Lord has the prerogative to provide instructions, and these are our absolute standards of right behavior. God's blessing on lives and nations comes through obedience to his commands. God said to Abraham, "In your seed all the nations of the earth shall be blessed, because you have obeyed My voice" (Gen. 22:18).

God gave us ten commandments that reveal both his character and ours. Thus, while he is seen to be holy, we are sinful. These commands were given on *two* tablets of stone because they concern first our relationship to God, and second our relationship to fellow humans. As revealed in Exodus 20:2–17, God's abiding commandments are:

(1) I am the LORD your God. . . . You shall have no other gods before Me.

(2) You shall not make for yourself any carved image, or any likeness of anything that is in heaven above, or that is in the earth beneath, or that is in the water under the earth; you shall not bow down to them nor serve them. . . .

(3) You shall not take the name of the LORD your God in vain, for the LORD will not hold him guiltless who takes His name in vain.

(4) Remember the Sabbath day, to keep it holy. . . .

(5) Honor your father and your mother. . . .

(6) You shall not murder.

(7) You shall not commit adultery.

(8) You shall not steal.

(9) You shall not bear false witness against your neighbor.

(10) You shall not covet your neighbor's house . . . nor anything that is your neighbor's.

God's authority and power is absolute. He therefore has the right to speak and to be obeyed.

A Convicting Voice

Having created and commanded, one of the first words the Lord spoke to his creation was to convict them of disobedience. Satan had intervened in the Garden of Eden—questioning, adding to, taking away, and changing the things that God had said. Man was made so intricately in the image of God that the least flaw would change him into the image of the devil. Far from becoming like gods (as the devil promised), after their sinful disobedience Adam and Eve sought to run away from God. Tenderly and compassionately, God spoke with convicting words: "And they heard the sound of the Lord God walking in the garden. . . . [He said:] 'Where are you?'" (Gen. 3:8–9). Despite their excuses, how deeply ashamed these first humans must have felt! Their intimacy with God had gone. Theirs was a paradise lost.

Centuries later, God's voice spoke again, this time through his prophets—repeatedly saying to his people, "You have not obeyed the voice of the Lord." Those who do business with God will feel the loathsomeness of sin whenever they hear his convicting voice.

A Converting Voice

Yet God does not leave us without hope, for his voice speaks also of redemption: God delights to demonstrate his power by turning people from their sinful ways. As a doctor diagnoses an illness before bringing about a cure, so God convicts people of their sin, not to leave them wallowing in the mire of introspective guilt, but to bring them to a place of forgiveness and new life in himself. Centuries ago Saul of Tarsus found this out most dramatically. When Saul set out on a trail of havoc and disaster, God arrested him in his tracks and spoke. Saul fell to the earth and "heard a voice saying to him, 'Saul, Saul, why are you persecuting Me?'"

(Acts 9:4). He was never to be the same again. Saul became Paul, a pattern-saint for all who would follow Christ.

The hymnwriter Horatius Bonar described his own quite-different conversion:

> I heard the voice of Jesus say,
> "Come unto Me and rest;
> Lay down, thou weary one, lay down
> Thy head upon My breast."
> I came to Jesus as I was,
> Weary, and worn, and sad;
> I found in Him a resting place,
> And He has made me glad.

Have you heard the converting voice of God as it appeals to you to trust Jesus Christ as your Savior?

A Calling Voice

There is a sense in which we are both commanded and called to follow Jesus Christ. God calls us to believe and trust his Son and then to serve him. However, the Christian life is not haphazard, since God has a plan and a pattern for each of us. He gives talents and abilities for Christians to use for his glory. Fullness of joy is experienced by the person who is right with God and ready to serve him in whatever way *God* chooses.

The Lord may be calling you to be saved. The Bible tells us: "Today, if you will hear His voice, do not harden your hearts . . ." (Heb. 3:7–8; cf. Ps. 95:7–8). He may be calling for service, such as when Moses was called at the burning bush or Isaiah after King Uzziah's death; or he may simply be wanting you to commune deeply with him, as when he says, ". . . If anyone hears My voice and opens the door, I will come in to him and dine with him, and he with Me" (Rev. 3:20). In each case, the good news is that God calls and speaks to us individually.

If you have trusted Jesus Christ, are you certain that you are exactly where he would have you be at this time? If not, ask him either to confirm it in your heart or to call you to another sphere of service. "The steps of a good man are ordered by the LORD" (Ps. 37:23a)—but so are the *stops!*

A Calming Voice

Suffering is one of the inevitable marks of humanity. Yet the God who speaks is also the God who sees all. Whatever turmoil you may be suffering physically, emotionally, or spiritually, God can calm your heart as he speaks to soothe the hurt and pour balm into the wounds. The fiery prophet Elijah was physically and mentally drained after the great conquest over the prophets of Baal at Mount Carmel. The very next day, when the evil Jezebel threatened to kill him, he could not cope. Elijah deserted his duty and fled a day and a half's journey into the wilderness, wishing himself dead. God compassionately fed him and gave him sleep. And then God spoke, not through a wind or earthquake or fire, but through a "still small voice" (1 Kings 19:12). He set Elijah back on the path to being restored. God cares and, unlike humans, he can cope with anything! Whatever your need, he lovingly appeals to you to trust in his strength and caring.

A Coming Voice

The final chapters of world history will not be written by politicians or controlled by some person pushing a button to create a world holocaust. There is coming a day when the voice of God will be heard above the clamor of the many other voices crying for attention today. The Old and New Testaments assure us of God's ultimate victory over all the powers of this world. "The LORD also will roar from Zion, And utter His voice from Jerusalem; The heavens and earth will shake . . ." (Joel 3:16). The apostle Paul wrote, "For the Lord Himself will descend from heaven with a shout, with the voice of an archangel, and with the trumpet of God . . ." (1 Thess. 4:16). Those who have ignored God throughout life will hear the clear voice of God in the end times. In fact, even the dead will hear his voice. One day all creation will hear God's roar again.

The Voice of Christ

God the Creator revealed himself to us through his Word, the Bible. Thousands of times we read there, "Thus says the Lord," or "The Lord said . . ." The Bible is God-breathed, and divinely inspired. Therefore it is absolutely trustworthy.

The Bible is God's written Word and Jesus is God's living, loving Word. Both were given to us by God, using mankind as his instrument. The Bible is God's Word, though penned by human hands; likewise was Jesus fully God, though conceived and born through the virgin Mary. It is one of God's great mysteries that both are fully of God and fully of man. All that Jesus spoke and did was part of God's revelation to man. God may speak to people through his creation or their conscience or the conversion of someone else, but he speaks primarily through Christ and Holy Scripture.

The voice of Jesus the Son is the voice of God the Father. Just as God's voice is like the sound of many waters, so is Christ's voice.

Jesus' voice is *creative*. As he gave thanks for the loaves and fishes, he broke them and fed thousands. There was ample food and some left over.

God's is a *commanding* voice, and so is Christ's. He gave us new commandments, applying Old Testament laws to individuals and saying that we should love our enemies, pray for our persecutors, turn the other cheek, and so on.

Christ *convicts* us, too. Though he severely condemned sin, especially religious hypocrisy and pride, his desire was always to bring individuals to a place of humble repentance and trust in his salvation. He came not to condemn the world but that it might be saved through him.

The Son of God *converts* both the self-sufficient and the deliberately sinful. The woman at the well needed Christ. She had had five husbands and was now living with another man. Religious Nicodemus, a ruler of the Pharisees, also needed Jesus. Christ's voice speaks with converting power.

Jesus *calls*. Some of his first recorded words are those to the fishermen: "Follow Me."

Christ's voice *calmed* the troubled sea and brought tranquility even to the demoniac who lived among the tombs.

Christ's is also a voice of expectation. He has said, "Surely, I am *coming* quickly."

Like many streams merging into one, so all these voices are heard at the cross. The work of creation was superseded by the act of re-creation that Christ was working on the cross. Creation, the Bible says, was the work of God's fingers, salvation the work of God's arm. Christ cried out on the cross, "It is finished," meaning that his work of dying for the sin of the world was accomplished. The sin of our breaking the commandments that God had given was laid on Jesus. It is because of his sacrificial death that he could pray, "Father, forgive them." He now calls us to follow him.

All humanity was represented at the foot of the cross—a worthy woman: Mary, his mother; the cynical, mocking Roman soldiers; a good young man: John, the beloved disciple; and the dying thief who trusted Christ and would have knelt at the cross if he could. Everyone needs to be at the place of recognizing that forgiveness was purchased by Jesus. Peace and redemption were provided at the cross, and that is to be remembered regularly by Christians in the breaking of bread and drinking the cup of the Lord's death until he comes again in glory.

Early in the biblical record, God's voice is heard asking, "Where are you?" God's final message is recorded near the end of Scripture: "And I heard a loud voice from heaven saying, 'Behold the tabernacle of God is with men, and He will dwell with them, and they shall be His people, and God Himself will be with them and be their God'" (Rev. 21:3).

Listen carefully, for God is speaking to *you*. His words will meet your need and, by drawing you to himself, make you a blessing to others. Will you obey his voice today?

2

Opportunity Beckons

> Remember now your Creator in the days of your youth (Eccles. 12:1).

What do you do when you have everything? What do you do when you have nothing?

Is it not strange how people who apparently have everything often find that they have nothing! A friend of mine brought himself from poverty to great wealth but then admitted to me, "When I was young I dreamed that one day I would have a lovely family and a silver Rolls-Royce and be a multimillionaire. I am thirty-two now and have acquired those things, but I am neither happy nor satisfied with my wealth."

The Roads to Disappointment

We so often say, "Money cannot buy happiness." But deep down doesn't everyone seem to believe that he or she would be the exception to that rule? We never seem to learn that nothing in this world truly satisfies. Centuries ago King Solomon wrote the Book of Ecclesiastes, showing how he learned the truth of that lesson. He had great power and wealth, and yet he felt bitter disappointment. Each road he traveled turned out to be a cul-de-sac—a dead end in a maze of worldly allures.

Highway of Knowledge. Solomon wrote: "And I set my heart to seek and search out by wisdom concerning all that is done under heaven. . . . [I said,] 'Look, I have attained greatness, and have gained more wisdom than all who were before me in Jerusalem. My heart has understood great wisdom and knowledge.' . . . I perceived that this also is a grasping for the wind. . . . he who increases knowledge increases sorrow" (Eccles. 1:13, 16–18).

The Avenue of Hard Work. Solomon invested, he produced, and he built—and yet on reflection the king said: "Then I hated all my labor in which I had toiled under the sun, because I must leave it to the man who will come after me" (Eccles. 2:18).

Streets of Materialism and Pleasure. This king, this so-called wise man who had a thousand wives and everything he needed to gratify his flesh, wrote: "I searched in my heart how to gratify my flesh with wine. . . . I built myself houses, and planted myself vineyards. I made myself gardens and orchards . . . I made myself waterpools . . . I acquired male and female servants and had servants born in my house. Yes, I had greater possessions of herds and flocks than all who were in Jerusalem before me. I also gathered for myself silver and gold and the special treasures of kings and of the provinces. . . . Whatever my eyes desired I did not keep from them. . . . And indeed all was vanity and grasping for the wind. There was no profit under the sun (Eccles. 2:3–8, 10–11).

The Turnpike of Riches. Although Solomon enjoyed great wealth, he concluded that whatever a person's status, "As he came from his mother's womb, naked shall he return, To go as he came; And he shall take nothing from his labor which he may carry away in his hand" (Eccles. 5:15). A thousand or so years later, Jesus was to speak of the transitory nature of all that the world offers when he said to the Samaritan woman at the well: "Whoever drinks of this water will thirst

again, but whoever drinks of the water that I shall give him
will never thirst . . ." (John 4:13–14). Solomon had already
guessed at the truth of those words while he gradually discovered that every "thing" was a disappointment to him.

The king's conclusion was that one must "fear God and
keep His commandments, for this is the whole duty of man"
(Eccles. 12:13). What Solomon was really saying was that
the only treasure that truly satisfies is a right relationship
with God. And the time to establish that relationship is
today: "Remember now your Creator in the days of your
youth . . ." (Eccles. 12:1). Life rolls relentlessly onward, and
youth all-too-quickly becomes old age. Richard Needham
described the seven ages of man as "Spills, drills, thrills,
bills, ills, pills, wills!"

To emphasize our urgent need to be related to God,
Solomon elaborated in a poem (Eccles. 12:1–8).

> Remember now your Creator in the days of your
>   youth,
> Before the difficult days come,
> And the years draw near when you say,
> "I have no pleasure in them":
> While the sun and the light,
> The moon and the stars,
> Are not darkened,
> And the clouds do not return after the rain;
> In the day when the keepers of the house trem-
>   ble,
> And the strong men bow down;
> When the grinders cease because they are few,
> And those that look through the windows grow
>   dim;
> When the doors are shut in the streets,
> And the sound of grinding is low;
> When one rises up at the sound of a bird,
> And all the daughters of music are brought low;
> Also when they are afraid of height,
> And of terrors in the way;
> When the almond tree blossoms,
> The grasshopper is a burden,

And desire fails.
For man goes to his eternal home,
And the mourners go about the streets.
Remember your Creator before the silver cord is
      loosed,
Or the golden bowl is broken,
Or the pitcher shattered at the fountain,
Or the wheel broken at the well.
Then the dust will return to the earth as it was,
And the spirit will return to God who gave it.

"Vanity of vanities," says the Preacher.
"All is vanity."

The Race Against Time

In this passage Solomon gives two basic reasons for remembering the Creator.

Everyone Is Growing Old. Dana Robbins said that old age is "when actions creak louder than words." Yes, growing up soon gives way to growing old. In his poem, Solomon symbolically describes an old man. Youth is a time when "the clouds do not return after the rain," but in old age "the keepers of the house tremble"—our hands shake and grow feeble.

"The strong men bow down" speaks of legs that cannot now keep straight and upright. "The grinders cease" surely speaks of the teeth! Then difficulties with vision are described: "And those that look through the windows grow dim." Even talking and listening grows tiresome when "the doors are shut in the streets."

Old people often awake early—they rise up "at the sound of a bird." Yet, whereas music is a vital key to life for youth, "all the daughters of music are brought low" for elderly folk who find it difficult to distinguish sounds and voices. They are also afraid of heights—and terrors are in the street, says Solomon. (Muggings are obviously not a thing of this day and age alone.) Solomon even describes the color of an old man's hair. "The almond tree blossoms," surely describes the hair which has turned white (if not completely gone!). Even a "grasshopper is a burden"—the least thing weighs heavily on an old person's mind.

The ideal time to know and serve God is not in old age when "desire fails," but in youth! When appetites, abilities, and ambitions are dying, it is almost too late to give one's all to God or even to appreciate the magnitude of his glory. When a great offer of future provisioning was made to Barzillai by King David, he refused, saying, "I am eighty years old, can I discover what is pleasant and what is not? Can I taste what I eat or drink? Can I listen to the voice of singing men and women?" (*see* 2 Sam. 19:31–35). Every tick of a clock, each new sunrise, every passing season, reminds us that we are all growing older. Having tried everything the world offers, Solomon says, "Remember *now* thy Creator. . . ." He also gives a further reason for such advice.

Everyone Is Going to Die. An attorney's advertisement reads: "Making a will won't kill you," reflecting the fact that everyone dreads death's inevitability. However, the Bible says that death is God's punishment for sin. If there had been no sin, there would have been no death. God had to say to Adam, "To dust you shall return." Today, every human being must take a solemn journey to that final destination.

Solomon, in his poem, expressed it like this: "For man goes to his eternal home." The grave is man's longest dwelling place on earth. "And mourners go about the streets" in Solomon's day and ours, but it makes no difference to the one who is deceased. Randolph Churchill, son of Sir Winston, once said that the only time he would hit the headlines would be when he died. However, he was wrong. Since he died on the same day that Robert Kennedy was assassinated, Kennedy took the headlines and Churchill made only a few lines in the middle pages! But what difference does it make whether one's death is newsworthy? Solomon's poem goes on to describe death in several ways:

"the silver cord is loosed"—that which joins body and soul together is severed.

"the golden bowl is broken"—that which holds the water of life breaks.

"the pitcher shattered at the fountain"—the ability to draw from the well of life is gone.

"the wheel is broken"—the heart, that which drives our life's blood, works no more.

Finally, to summarize it all, Solomon says that death is a separation in which the dust returns to the earth and the spirit returns "to God who gave it." When life ceases and our time on earth is over, it will be too late to come to know God. There are no second chances, for after death comes judgment.

How to "Remember" God

A rabbi was once asked by a follower, "When is the best time to repent?"

"Repent the day before you die," said the rabbi.

"But I don't know when I will die" was the reply.

"Repent *today* then!"

One day that opportunity will reach an expiration date. Life will be finished. The time to "remember" our Creator is, therefore, before old age and before death. There are three basic ways to do that:

1. *Repent of all that has offended a holy God.* Repentance is not just an emotion, not just a regretful "I'm sorry." It is a deliberate act of turning from wrong while trusting in Christ for forgiveness. Specifically, it means that the thief intends to live honestly; the drunkard, soberly; the immoral person, purely; and the ungodly person in a godly fashion. Repentance means acknowledging one's sin before God and asking for his help in avoiding wrongdoing in the future.

2. *Receive Christ as Savior and Lord.* Christ did not come into the world to call righteous people to himself, but to redeem sinners. When he died, he was actually carrying on his shoulders the sins of the world. Jesus took the punishment for *our* sin of forgetting our Creator, for rejecting God and his commandments. He died to make it possible for

guilty mankind to start again—remembering our relationship to God the Father.

The first person to trust in the crucified Christ's power was the dying thief who was crucified at his side. He prayed, "Lord, remember me when You come into Your kingdom" (Luke 23:42). In his act of asking the Lord to remember him, he was in fact recognizing and receiving the Lord. Christian conversion occurs when an individual truly turns from sin to trust Christ as his or her personal Savior and Lord. Although I have met people who have regretted the day of their physical birth, I have never met anyone who has regretted a spiritual "new birth." It is a wonderful thing to know that you are made right with God through the finished work of Christ on the cross. That is possible by simply allowing Christ into your life to forgive the past and guide your future.

3. *We must live for Christ.* Joy, satisfaction, and a deep knowledge of God are not in store for those who trifle with the things of eternity. We are not to give only the dregs of a day, a week, or a lifetime to Christ. He is worthy of our best—our wholehearted devotion and service—as we remember *now* our Creator.

3

Light and Life

> In Him was life, and the life was the light of men (John 1:4).

How sad that "life" for so many is darkness, while Jesus Christ brings both light and life for the asking. Those who trust Christ find that he changes death to eternal life and darkness to light. Christ, the Light of the World and the Prince of Life, reveals and releases the brilliance of his life-sustaining power. This is seen especially throughout the Gospel of John.

Bringing Life to Water. In John 2, we see that Christ gave "life" to water. What a disappointing moment it was when the wine ran out at the wedding in Cana. Yet Christ imparted life to ordinary water, turning it into premium wine that satisfied and made merry the hearts of the guests. Jesus' first miracle shines out to proclaim that *life with him is joyful.* Wine here represents happiness and joy. Jesus takes the commonplace and makes it rich with promise. He said, "I have come that they may have life . . . more abundantly" (John 10:10b). Christians are far from being miserable people, but each believer is daily learning true contentment and joy in Christ himself.

Bringing Life to People. In John 3, we read of religious Nicodemus' coming to Christ at nighttime to talk of spiritual matters. Jesus told him quite simply that he had to be born again if he was to have eternal life and enter the kingdom of God. Nicodemus was a Pharisee from Judea, but he found the secret of life in Christ. Later in John's Gospel (John 4), a wayward woman of Samaria met Jesus at a well. There at the well, as she trusted Jesus' words, she found life springing up like a well of water within her.

Still later, a nobleman's son was healed by the power of Christ. This incident led to the man's entire household believing in Jesus. The man was an influential person from Galilee, but he came to Christ for "life" (John 4:46–54). Jesus appealed to Nicodemus's mind, the Samaritan woman's conscience, and the nobleman's heart—but all with the intention that they might trust him.

There is clear light from these and other incidents that living *in Christ is to live a spiritual life.* The basic difference that Christ makes to those who believe in his Saviorhood is that they have a *new,* spiritual life. There then emerges a relationship with God that affects and alters all things: "For the wages of sin is death, but the gift of God is eternal life in Christ Jesus our Lord" (Rom. 6:23).

Bringing Life to the Helpless. John 5 relates how Christ gave life to previously "dead" legs! For many years a poor, infirm man had lain hoping that someone would dip him into the healing waters of the pool of Bethesda, but he had "no man" to help. Christ was more than mere "man." As God in human form, he had the power to heal when he said, "Rise, take up your bed and walk." Immediately the man received life in his legs. He walked away and picked up his bed, as if to show that he would never return to his former life of infirmity. The light from this incident is that *we have new life in Christ.* We "walk in newness of life" (Rom. 6:4). Christ does not just rearrange the old life; he carefully replaces it with a brand-new existence. Each new day the Christian has the privilege of walking with Christ and running his errands with joyful gratitude.

Bringing Life to Loaves and Fish. In John 6, we see Christ giving life to two dead fish and five loaves of bread! In so doing he sets a threefold example for all to follow: (1) he gave thanks—it is right, as well as a good testimony, to say grace before all meals; (2) he amply fed the hungry—Jesus met physical and spiritual needs; and (3) he gathered the leftovers—wasting food when so many are hungry is unthinkable for Christ and his followers.

What light is there from this miracle? Jesus told us the answer when *he called himself "the bread of life."* True life cannot be found anywhere but in him and by regularly feeding on him. Christ is to be our daily delight. Reading his Word and communing with him in prayer provides a sufficient supply of strength to meet every trial and test.

Bringing Life to a Fallen Woman. In John 8, Christ gave life to a woman who had been caught in the act of adultery. The religious leaders who said that she must by law be stoned, were seeking to trap Jesus in a "wrong" decision. Their attitude was completely at fault, as was their action in bringing only the woman, not the guilty man, for judgment. Jesus wrote in the dust, perhaps fulfilling Jeremiah 17:13b—"'Those who depart from Me shall be written in the earth, because they have forsaken the LORD, the fountain of living waters.'" Christ appealed to the crowd: "He who is without sin among you, let him throw a stone at her first" (John 8:7). Then from the oldest to the youngest, they left the scene. Christ did not condemn this woman but commanded her to go and sin no more.

What a wonderful encounter! Here, too, is light. *Christ is our justification.* Through him, "the free gift came to all men resulting in justification of life" (Rom. 5:18). At a Christian's moment of conversion there is cleansing from sin, justification before God, and the start of a life in, for, and with Jesus Christ our Lord and Savior.

Bringing Life to the Blind. John 9 shows us that Christ gave life to "dead" eyes. Here, a man born blind rejoiced to see the Christ who had anointed his eyes. There was now blazing new light and bounteous life for this man. Again we are shown that Christ is the Light of the World. He has promised to all who will follow him that they will not walk in darkness. The exciting journey with Jesus Christ is not dependent on new experiences, excitements, or excesses but on his presence alone. *He is the light of life.* All others bring darkness and delusion.

Bringing Life to Lazarus. John 11 details for us Jesus raising Lazarus, who had been dead and buried for four days. Christ wept at the tomb, thus identifying himself with all human sorrow. Then he called, "Lazarus, come forth!" Bound in graveclothes, but very much alive, the body that had been dead and beginning to decay came out from his tomb. Christ gave life to a dead man. In so doing, he revealed to us that *he is "the resurrection and the life"* (John 11:25). For every believer there is the promise of eternity. Though a Christian dies physically, he is more alive than ever! To be free from sin, sorrow, separation, and death is the prospect of all who turn in repentance and faith to the Savior.

Bringing Life to Barabbas. In the final stages of Christ's earthly ministry, he again demonstrated the truth of "in Him was life and the life was the light of men." All four Gospels attest that Jesus in effect gave life to Barabbas, his fellow prisoner. The name *Barabbas* means "son of my father." He was like us all—sons and daughters of our fathers—having done wrong, and deserving to die. Christ died in place of Barabbas and us. There is a bright beaming light from this episode, too. *Christ's is a saving life.* It is through his death that we have life. When he died he was actually paying the penalty for all of our sins, providing the only way of forgiveness for us all. Only when we cling to the "old, rugged cross," confessing our sin and trusting Christ, can we find God and new life. Paul said, "I have been crucified with Christ; it is no longer I who live, but Christ lives in me . . ." (Gal. 2:20).

Bringing Life to Himself. In John 20 comes the ultimate miracle: Christ gave life to his own dead body. In every great act of God, the Trinity (the one true God, in three persons—Father, Son, and Holy Spirit) is at work—in the creation and in the incarnation, baptism, death, and resurrection of Jesus Christ. We read in Scripture that the Father raised up Christ (1 Cor. 6:14), that the Spirit raised him up (Rom. 8:11), and also that Christ raised himself (John 2:19). Neither the grave nor the guards could keep Jesus in the tomb. He defeated sin and death. The light shed by this great event is that Christ's life is eternal. So, too, do Christians look beyond the grave: "For as in Adam all die, even so in Christ all shall be made alive. . . . The last enemy that will be destroyed is death" (1 Cor. 15:22, 26).

Alexander Whyte said "the Christian life is a series of new beginnings." If you have never recognized the life and light offered by Jesus Christ, ask him now to forgive your sins on the basis of his death for you. Ask him to live in you and through you on the basis of his resurrection. Then, as a believer, you will have the privilege and duty of "holding forth the word of life" (Phil. 2:16). Jesus said, "Let your light so shine before men that they may see your good works and glorify your Father in heaven" (Matt. 5:16).

4

Sin's Progression

Who is the man that fears the LORD? Him shall He teach in the way He chooses (Ps. 25:12).

Sitting side by side in school classrooms are pupils who will someday accomplish great things for good—and others for evil. Karl Marx and the great preacher C. H. Spurgeon apparently studied at the same time in the British Museum. So, too, did John the Baptist and Herod Antipas live and work during the same period of history. Both were swayed by the past as they worked out a future for themselves. Both were very close to the greatest moments of world history—when Jesus lived, died, and rose again. They basically believed in the same God and were familiar with his Law. They were both mere humans and thus were going to either heaven or hell. Both were even sometimes found under the same roof, but there the similarity ceases.

For Herod himself had sent and laid hold of John [the Baptist], and bound him in prison for the sake of Herodias, his brother Philip's wife; for he had married her. For John had said to Herod, "It is not lawful for you to have your brother's wife." Therefore Herodias held it against him and wanted to kill him, but she could not; for Herod feared John, knowing that he was a just and holy man, and he protected him. . . . Then an opportune day came when Herod on his birthday gave a feast for his nobles, the high officers, and the chief men of Galilee. And when Herodias' daughter herself came in and danced, and pleased Herod and those who sat with him, the king said to the girl, "Ask me whatever you want, and I will give it to you." . . . So she went out and said to her mother, "What shall I ask?" And she said, "The head of John the Baptist!" Immediately she came in with haste to the king and asked, saying, "I want you to give me at once the head of John the Baptist on a platter." And the king was exceedingly sorry; yet. . . . he did not want to refuse her. And immediately the king sent an executioner [who] . . . beheaded him in prison, brought his head on a platter, and gave it to the girl; and the girl gave it to her mother (Mark 6:17–22, 24–28).

Herod Antipas was the ruler of two provinces, including Galilee. He was the eldest son of the infamous Herod who had ordered the killing of all baby boys under the age of two in Bethlehem, at the time of Jesus' birth. However, this Herod was not responsible for the sins of his father. This Herod had married a princess and was "a builder," having constructed the city of Tiberias. He enjoyed listening to the preaching of John the Baptist. Although John denounced specific sins, maybe Herod delighted in having the sins of *others* preached against. Of course, he wanted to keep his own sins intact without being criticized!

Let us examine the progress of sin in Herod's life.

First, *sin captures the person.* Herod was living at ease in a position of honor. Nothing stood in the way of his obtaining pleasure. On a trip to Rome he became infatuated with his brother's wife, Herodias. No doubt she was beautiful and great fun to be with, but when God gave the commandment, "You shall not commit adultery" there were no exceptions to those five words! Even if Herod consulted with others to obtain their advice, there were few men brave enough to rebuke the king.

Each of us is born with a sinful nature. All children born

of a father and mother since Adam have been born tainted by sin. They are cut off from God. Since their very nature is in rebellion against God, they sin.

The Bible describes sin in differing ways. In 1 Kings 8:47, Solomon's prayer describes sin as having "done wrong . . . committed wickedness." Sin can have the meaning of "missing the mark," "disobeying," or "deliberately failing to conform to a true standard." Sin in Old Testament terms is the refusal to obey God's ten commandments, which summarize his requirements for mankind. And we are all guilty!

As soon as an individual begins to tolerate a specific sin, there is trouble. Just as certain "minor" diseases can eventually debilitate the whole body, sin spoils every part of our being. It spreads and increases, hardening and polluting our being. Entering a course of sin is often like buying a one-way ticket to disaster. Authorities once set to work to clean up Sir Walter Scott's statue in Edinburgh. No matter how hard they tried, the statue remained dirty-looking. Then they found that the stone itself was dark-colored, and no amount of scrubbing would ever change that! How like human nature—grimy in appearance and character! Sin took firm hold of Herod once he fell into adultery!

Sin Kills the Conscience. The Greeks define conscience as "the pain you feel when you do wrong." John Trapp said, "Conscience is God's spy and man's overseer." However, since it is possible to silence one's own conscience, it is not always an accurate guide to proper behavior. Herod chose sin rather than a clear conscience.

There was no way that Herod's adultery was ever to be right, and the Baptist plainly said so. Herod in turn locked up John—just like the man who, on reading that smoking causes lung cancer, gave up reading! John straightforwardly reproved Herod, but the ruler's new wife had it in for John and wanted to kill him. If we continue in wrongdoing, it is possible to so harden our hearts that our awareness of sin no longer hurts, even though the sin itself is damaging our souls. John, the innocent one, was now in prison—while guilty Herod was free.

Sin Courts Evil Companions. Those who do wrong quickly seek like-minded companions. Sinful but indecisive Herod had aligned himself with a vengeful wife, Herodias, who plotted with other evil people to have John silenced. Eventually her "opportune day" arrived (though *any* day provides an opportunity for doing either good or evil).

A party was arranged. Festivities are not wrong in themselves, but very often they lead to a raising of passion and lowering of inhibitions. Dancing can be either sensual or spiritual, but virtually every time dancing is mentioned in the Bible, someone fell into sin as a direct or indirect result of that dancing. That is not in the Bible accidentally, but as a warning. Herodias was herself evil, but—even worse—she taught her daughter to do wicked things. Herod was a weak man who had already broken the seventh commandment by committing adultery. The sixth, "You shall not murder," is not going to be kept for long! Salome, Herodias's daughter, danced to please this weak ruler. She used her body to sensually stir Herod and the guests. So carried away was Herod that he made a rash vow, swearing, "Whatever you ask me, I will give you. . . ." He was ready to give half his kingdom (Mark 6:23). In contrast, Jesus said, "For what will it profit a man if he gains the whole world, and loses his own soul?" (Mark 8:36). The value of a human soul is greater than anything in this world, but Herod was about to sell his soul to keep face with those who had heard his foolish promise.

Salome went back and asked her mother what she should say to Herod. Callously her mother asked for the head of John on a platter. Herod, who was guilty of making a rash vow, was even more guilty because he kept it. Twisted values indeed! He killed a prophet to keep a vow made in passion. Evil companions encourage each other in their sinning.

Sin Condemns Its Victims. Basically, Herod's achievements are forgotten, but one day of passion, excess, and crime remained in the memories of all, including himself. His guilty conscience, like a hibernating serpent just waiting for the warmth needed to end its slumber, awaited its chance to awaken and accuse. Herod may have gotten rid of John, but the Baptist's voice still thundered in his mind.

Who had been responsible for John's execution? Was it Herod, Herodias, Salome, or the actual executioners? Herod knew the answer. On hearing later of the work and words of Jesus Christ, who was still ministering, Herod said, "This is John, whom I beheaded; he has been raised from the dead!" (Mark 6:16). Herod was haunted not by John but by his own guilt. But what a strange thing for Herod to say! Herod was a Sadducee and therefore did not believe in life after death. But every heart knows better than that since the hope for eternity is indelibly written on all our inner beings. I remember an atheistic lawyer arrogantly saying on the radio, "I'd like to ask God a few questions!" How could he say that when he claimed not to believe in God?

Beware of sin's defilement. It blinds, deafens, and deadens the soul. Sin ultimately condemns its victims both in life and in eternity.

Sin Crucified Christ. Herod was gradually mastered by his self-indulgence and became totally unrepentant. On the eve of the crucifixion, Jesus was sent to Herod, who was curious and eager to meet him. After all, reports of all that Christ had done would have reached the palace. Stories such as the feeding of the thousands, the many healings, and other miracles would have been much talked about.

And Christ the prisoner was sent to Herod for trial! Herod must have clapped his hands with glee. Perhaps he might now see a miracle if the "magic-worker" would perform for him. He was delighted. He turned to Christ to examine him, but Jesus spoke volumes through silence, not words. Jesus was silent so that the voice of the Baptist could be heard, he who had said of Jesus: "I have seen and testified that this is the Son of God" (John 1:34). However, one must be careful not to silence for voice of God. "The Spirit of God shall not strive with men forever" (Gen. 6:3). Jesus had once called Herod, "that fox" (Luke 13:32), and for this sly, sinister man there was now no escape from his sinful ways. As Christ's eyes penetrated Herod's confident facade, the proud ruler grew uncomfortable. Then his real self and evil nature came to the fore. We read, "Then Herod, with his men of war, treated Him [Christ] with contempt and mocked Him, arrayed Him in a gorgeous robe, and sent him back to Pilate" (Luke 23:11). Herod even befriended his arch-enemy Pilate as they united in the common cause of rejecting the God who had made them. Together they sent Christ to the cross. Two weak sinners condemned the Omnipotent One, who willingly and voluntarily allowed himself to suffer for our sakes.

The Challenge

Here lies our hope! When Christ was crucified, it was the fulfillment of God's plan. Christ died to bear the condemnation of sinners' wrongdoing. God's Son, who had no sin, "bore our sins in His own body on the tree, that we, having died to sins, might live for righteousness . . ." (1 Peter 2:24).

> All my sin of every kind
> All the thoughts that stain the mind
> All the evil I designed
> . . . laid on Him
>
> All the ways my feet have strayed
> All the idols I have made
> All the times I have not prayed
> . . . laid on Him
>
> All the told and acted lies
> All success and all the tries
> Sins that I legitimize
> . . . laid on Him
>
> All that sinks me in the mire
> All the times of base desire
> All that needs a cleansing fire
> . . . laid on Him
>
> All my misdirected powers
> All my many wasted hours
> All my dreams of Ivory Towers
> . . . laid on Him

All that makes my spirit cold
All that keeps me from the fold
All that dims my Father's gold
. . . laid on Him

All the times I've grieved the Spirit
All the nature I inherit
All the punishment I merit
. . . laid on Him

Laid on Him, God's own dear Son,
Laid on Him, the Holy One,
Blotting out the noonday sun
When laid on Him.

                                    Lance Pibworth

Because Christ has died and risen again, he reverses the progression of sin. Christ confronts sinners with two alternatives: to stay in their sin and be lost eternally or to leave their sin and have life everlasting. Those who trust Christ find that he quickens the conscience. It becomes a lively judgment seat within, but it always points us back to the Word of God as the absolute standard of right and wrong. Your companions change when Christ is living within you. If you visit old haunts, there is a sense of "not belonging," and your greatest desire for old friends is that they might trust Christ as Savior and Lord, coming to know him as you have.

Because Christ has died, a sinner is no longer inevitably lost forever. Christ clears the culprit of guilt and offers salvation. "For God did not send His Son into the world to condemn the world, but that the world through Him might be saved" (John 3:17). God justifies the sinner on the grounds that Christ has paid the penalty. Before each of us is the choice: sin or the Savior? Which will it be for you? Accept the opportunity that Jesus Christ has provided by turning from the progression of sin in your life, and trusting him as your Savior and Lord.

5

Hidden Problems, Hidden Faith

. . . if you confess with your mouth the Lord Jesus and believe in your heart that God has raised Him from the dead, you will be saved (Rom. 10:9).

Don't we all hate being interrupted? According to a well-circulated story, one day Randolph Churchill was talking to his father when Sir Winston interrupted him. Randolph spoke again, only to receive the reply, "Don't interrupt me when I'm interrupting!"

Jairus must have felt similarly annoyed with a certain woman who came to Jesus with a hidden problem, especially since Jairus's little girl was only barely alive and he needed Christ's immediate help. Yet this woman drew Jesus' attention away from Jairus and interrupted the petition of this "ruler of the synagogue." We find the woman's story in Luke 8:41–48:

And behold, there came a man named Jairus, and he was ruler of the synagogue. And he fell down at Jesus' feet and begged Him to come to his house, for he had an only daughter about twelve years of age, and she was dying. But as He went, the multitudes thronged Him. Now a woman, having

a flow of blood for twelve years, who had spent all her liveli-
hood on physicians and could not be healed by any, came
from behind and touched the border of His garment. And
immediately her flow of blood stopped. And Jesus said, "Who
touched Me?" When all denied it, Peter and those with him
said, "Master, the multitudes throng You and press You, and
You say, 'Who touched Me?'" But Jesus said, "Somebody
touched Me, for I perceived power going out from Me." Now
when the woman saw that she was not hidden, she came
trembling; and falling down before Him, she declared to Him
in the presence of all the people the reason she had touched
Him and how she was healed immediately. And He said to
her, "Daughter, be of good cheer; your faith has made you
well. Go in peace."

Jesus was used to interruptions. He saw each one as an
opportunity instead of an intrusion. For example, when
Jesus was speaking in one crowded house, a paralytic was
lowered through the roof to meet with him. While Jesus
spoke to his disciples, a man interrupted to ask Jesus to
speak to his brother about dividing their inheritance.
Another time, when Christ was asleep in their boat, the disciples awoke him, fearful that the storm that had arisen
would wreck them all. Even when Jesus was praying, the
disciples interrupted him, saying that everyone was looking
for him. Only days before Christ's crucifixion, while on his
way to Jerusalem, he was interrupted by blind Bartimaeus,
who shouted out for help and healing.

Haste is a characteristic of people with limited power and
man-made priorities. Jesus, who followed a divine timetable
and had limitless resources, took each interruption as an
opportunity to serve and to teach. After all, Christ came for
people with needs.

Jairus was an important person, a man of influence who
commanded respect, yet who fell at Jesus' feet when his
daughter became ill. Jairus begged Jesus to come with him.
The request was urgent; no time could be wasted. But it was
at such a desperate moment that Jesus allowed a woman to
interrupt. (Later we read that Jesus' delay was followed by

a double blessing, for Jairus's pleas for his daughter's healing were also answered [*see* Luke 8:49–56]).

Hidden Problems

The poor lady in the passage above had suffered from a chronic flow of blood for twelve years. She probably felt weak and lethargic most of the time. Since she had busied herself in visiting every doctor available and paying dearly for their services, she had lost both her health and her wealth. Even worse, with this particular illness she was unfit for physical intimacy and was also ceremonially "unclean," thus curtailing spiritual life as well. Furthermore, there seemed no hope or sign of healing and cure. In so many ways this lady is like most of us. A hidden problem affecting social, spiritual, physical, and emotional well-being lies in everyone—the deadly plague of sin! We have suffered the debilitating inroads of sin longer than the woman, and our multiplicity of plans to deal with the problem have been as useless as her consulting one doctor after another.

Human effort, no matter how valiant, is pitifully inadequate for procuring forgiveness of sin or power over evil. Picture Martin Luther, the brilliant scholar and monk. Imagine the sounds and sights in his monastery cell in Erfurt as portraying a man in conflict. He has tears, prayers, hunger, lacerations of the flesh—but all in the vain pursuit of a clear conscience before God. Luther wrote, "I was nothing the better but rather the worse." He even traveled to the Sancta Scala steps in Rome as a pilgrim, climbing and crawling on his bare knees in hopes that the burden of sin would roll off his back. Instead it weighed heavier as he climbed higher. Finally, according to tradition, he remembered the text that rang like heaven's music in his ears: *The just shall live by faith.* He rushed from the scene rejoicing, not in his own efforts, but in the finished work of Christ. As Scripture says, "For by grace you have been saved through faith, and that not of yourselves; it is the gift of God, not works, lest anyone should boast" (Eph. 2:8–9). Likewise, it was only when the woman was at the end of her rope and had exhausted her own efforts that she came with her hidden problem to Christ.

Hidden Faith

One can imagine that poor woman pushing her way through the narrow streets of the busy city. The crowds were an obstacle, but she was suffering, and perhaps she knew that Jesus always showed sympathy to the blind, maimed, and needy. Her faith was hidden; so far it was unexpressed in word or action.

There has always been a kind of mass contact with Christ. In so-called Christian countries, one day in seven still finds the wheels of industry grinding to a halt and the doors of commerce closing on the Lord's Day. We remember Christ's birth at Christmas and his death and resurrection at Easter. Spires, belfries, and crosses speak of Christ everywhere. Much literature has absorbed Christian concepts; classical music has its Handel and Bach; and even modern pop sings about heaven and hell, or God and the devil. At church weddings we are reminded that Christ visited the wedding feast at Cana, and at funerals we are consoled by the immortal words of Christ: "I am the resurrection and the life." No wonder so many people feel that simply being born in a Christian country and into a church-going family is sufficient to make them Christians. However, mere contact with the symbols of Christendom does not necessarily bring about the personal relationship with Christ that is vital if one is to know him in a saving way.

There must be that "touch" with the finger of faith. Jesus himself touched many folk—the leper, the dumb man, Peter's mother-in-law, the servant whose ear had been cut off—but on this occasion it was the person in need who reached out and made contact. This touch affected both Jesus and the woman. As he felt power going out to her, she was immediately healed.

If the crowds had noticed this, they would have been

angry. Religious people would have criticized her actions, since her unclean state could have contaminated another simply by touch. Her inner faith in the Lord had given her an immediate cure, yet she did not want to be seen by anyone. Her faith had been as hidden as her problem, but when she touched Christ she found that neither was hidden after all.

Christ has the power to heal and God knows all the details of our lives. In museums I have often seen plates and pictures inscribed with the words, "Thou, God, seest me." These biblical words are both a comfort and a challenge. God knows the thoughts and actions of the secret recesses of our minds and bodies. Our problems are never hidden from him. There was nothing particularly mystical about the hem, or border, of Jesus' garment, but there is plenty of symbolism present here. Notice that the hem of the garment is:

1. *The finished part.* On the cross Christ triumphantly cried out, "It is finished." He had accomplished the great work of paying for the world's sin. He had been born to die. The completed hem signifies the finished work of Christ on the cross.

2. *The pierced part.* A needle pierces a garment to turn and hold up its hem. This reminds us that the crucified Christ was pierced. A crown of thorns was wedged on his brow; rough, rugged, Roman nails pierced his hands and feet. Eventually a sword pierced Christ's side. However, the cross will never be understood without grasping its hidden work—the fact that our sin pierced the very soul of Jesus. Sin has always been abhorrent to God. Jesus, the pure and holy Son of God, hated sin. On the cross God took the sins we have forgotten and those we wish we *could* forget; the sins of the past, present, and future; the sins we love and those for which we hate ourselves—and laid them all on the Lord Jesus. How this hurt! Like a dagger, sin pierced his heart and soul. He would have recoiled from sin, but love held him there as sin battered and bruised the clean-minded, purely spoken, and holy life of Christ.

3. *The vital part.* Just as the hem is vital to a garment's

wholeness, so is the cross of Christ to ours. Jesus spoke of the hour to come when he would die. So vital was that death that the apostle Paul wrote: "For I determined not to know anything among you except Jesus Christ and Him crucified" (1 Cor. 2:2). What is *your* view of Christ and the importance of the cross? Your answer will reveal your standing before God and your eternal destiny.

4. *The part touched only by bending.* Stooping as she made her way to Christ, this woman pictured the humble, burdened attitude of those who trust the Savior—"Nothing in my hand I bring, simply to thy cross I cling." Archbishop Temple wrote, "The only thing we contribute to our salvation is a load of sin." It is only when we realize that our state is desperate that we can come in submission to Jesus, pleading forgiveness from the One who delights to pardon and cleanse. Arrogance and pride have no place in the individual who would willingly bow heart and head before the mighty King Jesus, who was willingly crushed by our sins.

Into the Open . . .

Jesus said to the woman, "Daughter, be of good cheer; your faith has made you well. Go in peace." Such blessing was bestowed although she had come to him with selfish motives. All she wanted was healing. There is no hint of devotion to Jesus or desire to make his name known to others. For so many who come to Christ, the dominant motivation may initially not be altogether worthy. The drunkard simply wants to be sober; the lonely husband needs a new start in his family; the sinner wants to avoid spending eternity in hell. So they turn to Christ. Is that wrong? I do not think so.

A newborn baby is a bundle of const
hungry or thirsty or dirty—and so it c
until that love is gradually awakened by
it and meet its needs. At first the baby's
ish, but in time unselfish devotion sh
becomes an example for the child and

measure. A "newborn" Christian may not necessarily love the Savior at first, but as that believer learns to walk with Jesus Christ and cultivate the relationship, love for the Lord will strengthen and grow. God commands us to repent, and whatever our motives, feelings, or fears, all people everywhere need to obey that command and open their hearts to Christ. Eventually his perfect love for each individual will draw a warm love by way of response.

No problem is hidden to Christ; nor is a sincere faith. But Christ wants this faith brought into the open, just as when he turned to the crowd and asked, "Who touched me?" It was good for this woman as well as the people around that her faith and her cure became known. Public confession of faith in the Lord Jesus is of great importance. Jesus said, "For whoever is ashamed of Me and My words, of him the Son of Man will be ashamed when He comes in His own glory, and in His Father's, and of the holy angels" (Luke 9:26). Expression deepens an impression. Secret discipleship is a contradiction of terms.

At first everyone denied touching Christ's garment, but eventually (though tremblingly) the woman declared to him, in the presence of all the people, the reason she had touched him. Christ brought her "into the open" because he himself offers an "open door" to salvation. We read of his work that : ". . . this thing was not done in a corner" (Acts 26:26); and Jesus himself said, "I sat daily with you, teaching in the temple" (Matt. 26:55).

Christ's birth was open—angels announced the event to the shepherds, and a star led the Wise Men to leave their land and come to worship Christ. Jesus' teaching was open—thousands heard him, and there was nothing secret about what he said. Nor were there secret handshakes or ceremonies. His miracles were open and seen by many. Furthermore, Jesus was always available and ready to be questioned by the religious establishment and for the common people to hear him.

Even Christ's death was open for all to see. He was suspended between heaven and hell for all of earth to gaze on.

Only in the actual moments when the sin of the world was laid on him did God cover the scene with darkness. After Christ rose from the grave, the stone was rolled away—not to let Christ out but to let the world look in. Having bodily risen, Jesus appeared to the women, to two men walking on the road to Emmaus, to two and then ten and then eleven disciples, as well as to a crowd of over five hundred. He is the open Christ. Those who would truly come to the Savior must do so openly. Today, will you bring your hidden and innermost needs and sins to the Christ who gave himself for you? Will you openly trust him and find for yourself that faith in him makes you right with God?

6

Rich Man, Poor Man

[Jesus said:] "For judgment I have come into the world, that those who do not see may see . . ." (John 9:39).

While standing in a school assembly, I once heard the following passage from Luke read aloud to over a thousand pupils. I remember that a teacher of mathematics turned to me and whispered, "I never knew that was in the Bible." Read carefully these words . . .

[Jesus said:] "There was a certain rich man who was clothed in purple and fine linen and fared sumptuously every day. But there was a certain beggar named Lazarus, full of sores, who was laid at his gate, desiring to be fed with the crumbs which fell from the rich man's table. Moreover the dogs came and licked his sores. So it was that the beggar died, and was carried by the angels to Abraham's bosom. The rich man also died and was buried. And being in torments in Hades, he lifted up his eyes and saw Abraham afar off, and Lazarus in his bosom. Then he cried and said, 'Father Abraham, have mercy on me, and send Lazarus that he may dip the tip of his finger in water and cool my tongue, for I am tormented in this flame.' But Abraham said, 'Son, remember that in your lifetime you received your good things, and likewise Lazarus evil things; but now he is comforted and you are tormented. And besides all this, between us and you there is a great gulf fixed, so that those who want to pass from here to you cannot, nor can those from there pass to us.' Then he said, 'I beg you therefore, father, that you would send him to my father's house, for I have five brothers, that he may testify to them, lest they also come to this place of torment.' Abraham said to him, 'They have Moses and the prophets; let them hear them.' And he said, 'No, father Abraham; but if one goes to them from the dead, they will repent.' But he said to him, 'If they do not hear Moses and the prophets, neither will they be persuaded though one rise from the dead'" (Luke 16:19–31).

Some Christians believe this is a true story; others maintain it is a parable. Regardless, all of Christ's parables were stories that were meaningful to his listeners because they contained events which could actually happen. This story is a study in contrasts.

The Poverty of Wealth

1. *These men lived different lives.* I can see in my mind's eye the beautiful villa in which the rich man lived. It would be painted white, perhaps standing on a hill surrounded by exotic gardens all well irrigated by streams and pools. If you were invited to a meal with this rich man, you would probably count yourself privileged. A servant would greet your knock at the door and, as you entered, the sense of quietude and coolness would be instantly welcomed. You would be ushered to the dining room, its highly polished table covered with the finest food and drink in rich abundance. The dinner hours would quickly pass in sheer delight as you enjoyed the surroundings and the company. Eventually you would move from the table to the ballroom where you would laugh, dance, and make merry into the early hours. Wending your way home, your mind would be filled with memories of a wonderful evening.

When alone, this rich man had his business to see to as well as his library of scrolls and books to enjoy. He had everything *except* God, and apparently he was satisfied—although one thing irritated him. Of late a beggar covered with sores had been lying outside his gate. He was a disgusting sight, and dogs even came and licked his wounds. On the other hand, if the rich man had the slightest ailment, the finest physician came scurrying to tend him. Since everyone, including the doctor, bypassed the beggar, the poor man was so hungry that he would have welcomed the crumbs from the rich man's table. He was so thirsty that he craved the water he heard flowing in the fountain, so raggedly clothed that he dreamed of the fine purple in which the rich man was adorned. Yet the beggar knew God. His very name tells us that. Lazarus means, "In God I trust." Can we have any doubt that he had come to the moment in his life of conversion and commitment? He had nothing *except* God, but he was satisfied with the God who was real to him.

Which of these two men are you most like? Compared with so many people, we in the West are rich. Most of us have food, housing, and clothing in abundance. So far as material well-being is concerned, we are wealthy. But the question is deeper. Is Christ your all-in-all? Is he the most important part of your life? If everything except the Lord were to be taken from you, would you be content?

2. *These men died different deaths.* Birth and death are common experiences that unite rich and poor. ". . . it is appointed for men to die once . . ." (Heb. 9:27).

I can imagine the rich man sitting on his balcony surveying the tranquil scene, when suddenly two of his servants come running up the long drive and into the rear entrance of the house. They barge into his presence, eagerly wanting to share the news: "Sir, you know the beggar who has lain at your gate—the one you tried to have removed—he's dead!"

A smile would creep across the face of the rich man. "Are you sure?" he asks.

"Yes, we kicked his body and there was no movement at all. He's definitely dead."

"Good," he would reply. "Go and get some rags and wrap up the body. Drag it away and bury it. Just get rid of it."

Quickly they would obey, taking the body to a desert patch where they would dig a hole and deposit it in the ground.

There would be no marker to commemorate the place. The beggar's body was worthless in both life and death, as far as the rich man was concerned.

Jesus also told of the rich man's death. He omitted the details, but we may imagine them. Was this wealthy man murdered? Did he die of malaria, or heart failure? We do not know. Death comes in many ways, but the news of this aristocrat's death would spread like wildfire: "Have you heard? The rich man has died and the funeral is tomorrow."

Relatives who had shown no interest for years, would now be intrigued by the news and make their way to the funeral. The streets would be lined, and people might comment: "He was a good man. He gave to the temple authorities and paid for the market square, which is named after him." Nobody would remember how he ignored the poor beggar. Yet it is our attitude to others that is the proof of our attitude to God. This rich man evidently loved neither God nor man.

A golden hearse, pulled slowly by stately horses, carries the coffin containing the rich man's body. He had left all his worldly goods. He could take nothing with him. In the finest of cemeteries, his body is lowered into the ground. Eventually a tombstone is laid over the place, with the words: "Here lies the body of a rich man."

Notice, though, it is only the body that lies there. His soul has gone elsewhere. Paul prayed that "spirit, soul, and body be preserved blameless . . ." (1 Thess. 5:23). Each of us is more than a body. That part eventually decays and dies, but the spirit and soul will go on eternally, in either heaven or hell.

3. *These men experienced different eternities.* For the poor beggar, death was a sweet moment of relief and release. One moment his body was in torment; the next he was carried by the angels (no one can go to heaven on his or her own efforts) to a place of no suffering, no sin, no sorrow, no separation, no disease, and no death. Oh, how blessed was eternity for this man! He will be with the heavenly host who enjoy their God forever. Heaven is a real place and experience for those who have trusted Christ to take away sin.

How different was eternity for the rich man! His moments of luxury and leisure were very short-lived compared with the fate that awaited him at death. Jesus said, "How hard it is for those who have riches to enter the kingdom of God!" (Luke 18:24). The riches of this man were of no use now. Despite all his wealth, he had been poverty-stricken. He was utterly lost. Jesus said of him, "The rich man also died and in hell. . . ."

Before anyone is condemned to the torments of Hades, that person will have pushed aside all the obstacles that God has placed in the way. He or she would have to ignore the prayers of friends and family, Christian booklets and posters, the Word of God, his or her own conscience, and—especially—the fact of a crucified, now-risen Christ who lovingly longs that each one should turn to him.

In this story, the rich man began to pray (at last!). He asked for mercy. He prayed that Lazarus the beggar would bring him just a drop of water to cool his tongue. Why did he specify Lazarus? I believe the implication was: "Lazarus is a nobody and of no consequence; surely you can spare that beggar to help me."

Everyone in heaven is there because that person is precious to God. No one is insignificant in his eyes, but the rich man's prayer for mercy was sincere and earnest—and too late! If only he had prayed five minutes before his death, instead of after. God's judgment is both fair and final, so the reply came back from Abraham, "Son, remember. . . ." He was called a son because he was of the line of Abraham and as such should have known the commandments and would have been taught the Scriptures at the synagogue. He truly was a "son," yet he ignored his heritage.

It is the strange and mysterious work of God to remind people of their past. When God by his Holy Spirit is at work in our lives, he arrests us in our tracks and reminds us of our past. If you have ever been driving a car and looked in a mirror, only to see a blue flashing light, you will have been aware of a thousand and one questions flashing through your mind in an instant: "Was I speeding? Did I indicate to turn? What have I done wrong?" In a similar way, God stops us, making us aware of sin within. When God bids us to remember, the memory can be quite painful.

The voice from heaven explained to the rich man that it is impossible for anyone to pass from heaven to hell (not that any would want to) and none can ever pass from hell to heaven. There is no mention of "purgatory" here or elsewhere in the Bible, only a fixed eternal place of either bliss or banishment. Suddenly, as he began to remember, the rich man thought of those he had influenced—his five brothers. Whether an individual chooses to receive or to reject Christ, his decision often affects others—his family, children, and neighborhood contacts. So the rich man thought of his brothers. Surely he had taught them to ignore the Lord, to live for the moment and not eternity, to ignore the needs of men and women round about! I believe he began to panic with fear at the thought of their pointing an accusing finger at him throughout eternity. He begged "father Abraham" that at least he would send Lazarus to warn the brothers of this place of torment.

In life, the brothers had ignored Lazarus. Why should they take notice now? But the situation was so desperate that logic had gone. Anyway, the Lord of Glory does not simply act at the whim and wish of anyone. Abraham therefore said that God had already revealed himself to man through his Word, the Bible. His Word is sufficient witness to the truth that must be believed and lived.

So frenzied was this lost man that he pleaded, ". . . but if one goes to them from the dead, they will repent." Such an argument is based on the false view that it is lack of evidence that prevents people from believing. The evidence, however, *is* convincing. Christ did live, die, and rise again. It is not that people cannot believe, but that they will not. Jesus said that it was an evil and adulterous generation that seeks after signs, but that his resurrection from the dead would be the only sign given (*see* Matt. 12:39–40). Abraham replied in a similar way saying, "If they do not hear Moses and the prophets, neither will they be persuaded though one rise from the dead." The rich man was silenced. Jesus died and rose again, but many still will not believe.

How Jesus Was Unique

1. *Jesus lived a different life.* The life of Christ was not marred and tainted by regret. His was a life devoid of double standards, selfishness, or greed. The Son of God delighted to do his Father's will and kept a perfectly clear conscience before both God and men. He cared for and coped with the waifs and strays of society and was always at the disposal of those in need. Although never too busy to bypass the needs of individuals he always had time to spend with his Father in prayer and communion. His teachings and work were consistent, including his power over nature, disease, and death itself. This God-man was without sin, but came into the world to save sinners. His was an utterly unique life.

2. *Jesus died a different death.* Sin has brought death's inevitability to every man and woman. Christ, however, was without sin, but his death was for us all. He tasted death for everyone when on him was laid the sin of the world. His death was open, though the work he did when on the cross was hidden. Sin never polluted the heart of God's Son, but it crushed Christ-as-man, the heart of heaven.

3. *Jesus experienced a different eternity.* Because Christ has died and risen, a way has been opened whereby ordinary people—sinners all—can enjoy God in life and in eternity. We read in Luke's Gospel that Jesus said, ". . . there is joy in the presence of the angels of God over one sinner who repents" (Luke 15:10). Who is in the presence of the angels of God but Christ? He who once wept over sinners now rejoices when he sees one repenting and believing. Eternity is filled with the thrilling joy over sinners who have turned to Christ.

The Believer's Inheritance

1. *A Christian lives a different life.* The Bible says. ". . . if anyone is in Christ, he is a new creation; old things have

passed away; behold, all things have become new" (2 Cor. 5:17). Aims, affections and ambitions totally change when Jesus comes to live within the life of someone who trusts him as Savior. Life and language become new. New Christians find that they have rich spiritual lives and God has become precious. As they daily bring their lives under the control of God's standards, they begin to find a new outlook. They now see the world from God's perspective.

2. *A Christian dies a different death.* The final enemy is death, but for the Christian it is a defeated foe. Christ arose from the grave and now lives through those who are his. For the believer, death is but the doorway to heaven.

In March 1984, William McConnel, the deputy governor of the Maize Prison in Northern Ireland was shot to death outside his house as he left for work one morning. Three weeks before his murder, he had written a letter expressing a premonition of death that he had felt. He concluded by saying, "Finally, let no one be alarmed as to my eternal security. In March 1966, I committed my life, talents, work, and actions to Almighty God in sure and certain knowledge that however slight my hold on Him may have been during my years at school, university, and the prison service, His promises are sure and His hold on me complete. Nothing can separate me from the love of God in Christ Jesus our Lord." The letter was read at McConnel's funeral service.

"Christ can make a deathbed softer than downy pillows," said a dying youngster. The knowledge that sin has been forgiven, and that there is peace with God through the finished work of Jesus Christ, transforms one's life and death.

3. *A Christian experiences a different eternity.* Heaven is promised to all who repent and believe. It is not presumptuous to say, "I am going to heaven when I die." God in the Bible has promised a place of eternal joy to those who are his children. Have *you* trusted Christ? Has there come a moment in your life when you have committed yourself to him forever? If not, do it today.

7

The Rich Fool

[Jesus said:] "For what is a man profited if he gains the whole world, and loses his own soul? Or what will a man give in exchange for his soul?" (Matt. 16:26).

What would you say is your most precious possession? Is it something sentimental? Is it something of financial value? Maybe it has only social significance. Or perhaps it is something utterly trivial! However much a treasured belonging may be worth, there is something you own that is more valuable. That is your own soul!

We live in an age in which people seem to pay more attention to trivia than to the important issues of life. Trivial Pursuits (devised by two Canadian journalists in 1982) has become as popular as such older games as Monopoly and Scrabble. To play well, one must answer questions as inconsequential as: "Who died with more than 1,000 patents to his name?" or "How many tentacles does a squid have?" or "What was the name of Sir Isaac Newton's dog?" Hardly world-shattering! The games we play reflect the way we live, and this present age is characterized as having wrong values. People seek to live on substitutes for the "genuine article." In fact, they have done so ever since sin first entered the world. Jesus' parable of the rich fool concerns such a man:

Then one from the crowd said to Him [Jesus], "Teacher, tell my brother to divide the inheritance with me." But He said to him, "Man, who made Me a judge or an arbitrator over you?" And He said to them, "Take heed and beware of covetousness, for one's life does not consist in the abundance of the things he possesses." Then He spoke a parable to them, saying: "The ground of a certain rich man yielded plentifully. And he thought within himself, saying, 'What shall I do, since I have no room to store my crops?' So he said, 'I will do this: I will pull down my barns and build greater, and there I will store all my crops and my goods. And I will say to my soul, "Soul, you have many goods laid up for many years; take your ease; eat, drink, and be merry."' But God said to him, 'You fool! This night your soul will be required of you; then whose will those things be which you have provided?' So is he who lays up treasure for himself, and is not rich toward God" (Luke 12:13–21).

Plenty of Nothing

The subject of this story is a man who had plenty—all that money could buy. There is nothing wrong with material wealth as long as one is aware of its limitations. Money can buy a bed but not sleep, books but not brains, food but not an appetite, a house but not a home, medicine but not health. Money can also buy sinful pleasures—but it can never purchase salvation's peace.

Bing Crosby was once asked by the interviewer on a television show why he had such a calm and unruffled air. He reached into his pocket and pulled out an enormous wad of dollar bills. "That helps," he said. Perhaps he was only kidding, but less flippant and more philosophical observers have disagreed. Film star Bridget Bardot described herself as "uprooted, unbalanced, and lost in a world that seems mad." Long ago, King Solomon reflected on what he had gained for himself and described it all as "vanity of vanities." The same was true of the rich fool in this parable. He had plenty of everything but peace.

The Problem of Excess

Despite all his possessions, this man had a problem. He had so much, he did not know what to do with the excess! At the same time he gave no thought to the widows and orphans or others who were poor and needy. He was completely self-satisfied and self-indulgent.

The Bible says, "Give me neither poverty nor riches" (Prov. 30:8b). Paul wrote that one should be content, having food and clothing (1 Tim. 6:8). More than this is always a burden. Wealth and worry are forever wedded together.

A Formulated Plan

The rich man's problem was hidden (he merely "thought within himself"), but he revealed his plan. He would pull down his barns and build greater ones so that he could "eat, drink, and be merry." His idea was to hoard his own wealth, the very thing that caused his problem! His selfishness was such that six times he thought or spoke of "I," and he referred to "my barns," "my crops," "my goods," and "my soul." That last especially revealed his folly. Without doubt it was God who had given him everything, but he had forgotten the Giver of all good gifts. If it were not for God, he could never have had crops nor goods—nor a soul.

All the rich man's thinking and planning was based on the false assumption that time was on his side. Surely he would have admitted that no one lives forever, yet he lived his life as if he did not believe that. Even today, in the mad, greedy rush for luxury, comfort, and commerce, people base their lives on a lie. They live on temporary replacements and not realities. But the substitutes do not last, and the only One who really matters is ignored. Immediately after telling this parable, Jesus talked about worry. He said how needless, how useless, and how godless it was. Anxiety exists, however, because the structure of people's lives has not been built with the Lord as the foundation and "a treasure in the heavens" their goal.

A Personal Summons

God commands all people everywhere to repent of their sin. This is a personal call. The only voice one is to heed also calls that "time is up." When God calls someone "a fool," it must be a perfect assessment, for God never makes mistakes. The books of Psalms and Proverbs describe some of the attributes of a fool, and each one applies to this man. In Psalm 14:1 we read that "the fool has said in his heart, 'There is no God.'" The rich fool revealed this attitude by leaving God out of all his thinking, planning, and scheming. Psalm 74:18 says that "a foolish people" blasphemes God's name. We see that by talking of "*my* soul," this rich man had been guilty of such blasphemy. In Psalm 107:17 we read that fools are afflicted because of their transgressions. Proverbs 1:7 says that the fool despises wisdom, Proverbs 18:7 that he has destruction in his mouth, and Proverbs 21:20 that he spends foolishly true treasure. This "rich fool" was guilty on all counts. Proverbs 26:10 states the law of God that applied to this rich man: "The great God who formed all things gives the fool his hire and the transgressor his wages."

God knows not only the date of our birth but also the date of our death. One day we must all pass through the turnstile of death, the great interrupter. Personal ambition and involvement cease the moment God blows that final whistle. There is a day coming when the doctor will put down his stethoscope for the last time, the minister will preach his last sermon, the builder will pack away his tools forever, and the farmer will plow his field for the final sowing. That day hastens on. Time stands still for none of us.

The Bible speaks of the *quickness* of time. Life is "swifter than a weaver's shuttle" (Job 7:6), and "All flesh is grass . . . The grass withers, the flower fades . . ." (Isa. 40:6–7). If you ask an elderly person how long his life has seemed, even an octogenarian will probably say that it has raced by and that childhood is as yesterday. Time rushes by!

The Bible also notes how important is the *quality* of time.

Christians are told to "walk circumspectly, not as fools but as wise, redeeming the time, because the days are evil" (Eph. 5:15–16). Once a man heard a sermon in which all listeners were challenged to ensure that each relationship was right and that apologies were owed to no one. The man was so moved by what he heard that he went home to write a letter of apology to his mother, whom he had wronged many times over the years. A few days later he received an urgent call to visit his mother, who was very ill in a hospital across the country. The man rushed to her bedside, but she was unconscious and never recovered. Imagine his relief when, sorting through her things, he found his letter. It had evidently been opened and read, so this relationship had been mended just in time.

In contrast, I remember an older man in the Yorkshire Dales saying to me, "I'd give anything to have just five more minutes with my wife. I'd tell her first that I was sorry, and secondly, that I love her and always will. But she died suddenly after we had had a terrible fight." God has a timetable for each of us—even for the Lord Jesus, who said, "I must work the works of Him who sent Me while it is day; the night is coming when no one can work" (John 9:4).

We know from the Bible that the brevity of life raises the *question* of time. Human decisions affect eternity. Five minutes can wreck and ruin a life as well one's eternal destiny. Elijah asked the Israelites, "How long will you falter between two opinions? If the LORD is God, follow Him. But if Baal, then follow him" (1 Kings 18:21). The people tried to avoid choosing, but their indecision was in itself a rejection of God.

A person is not truly ready to live unless at all times he is ready to die. The great C. H. Spurgeon was once preaching on the subject of heaven. His eye kept being drawn to a motionless elderly lady in the congregation. Eventually Spurgeon called over one of the ushers to check that the lady was all right, but he found that she had died. While listening to a sermon on heaven, she had gone there herself! The rich fool had made no preparations to meet God. Are you ready for God's personal summons? Are *you* prepared for the moment when your time will be no more?

Paying the Price

News spread in a small town that a wealthy man had died. "How much did he leave?" came the inevitable question.

"Everything!" was the stark but wise answer.

The rich fool in this parable also lost everything. Most important of all, he paid a terrible price for his foolishness—his soul. Did he not realize that the risk of eternal loss is too great to gamble with? If one could accumulate all the fame, fortune, and friends in the world, they would be insignificant compared with the value of one human soul.

> To lose one's wealth is much
> To lose one's health is more
> To lose one's soul is such a loss
> That nothing can restore.

Crowds gathered by the thousands in the amphitheater of ancient Rome to watch Christians being thrown to the lions. Now both those Christians and the pagan crowds are gone. The thousands who heard John Wesley and George Whitefield have all died, as have the preachers themselves. Gone, too, are the multitudes who fought at Waterloo—both victors and vanquished. ". . . it is appointed for men to die once, but after this the judgment" (Heb. 9:27). This is true both of men of history and men of today. I have often asked people, "Where will you spend eternity?" Most have never thought about the issue or simply hope that everything will eventually be all right. Just as it would be foolish to go on a plane flight if you thought there would be a crash landing, so it is folly to go through life without making preparations to ensure that all will be well at your final destination.

Christ, too, had an hour of death. In fact, he was born as a man so he could die. Voluntarily he went to the cross to take on himself all the folly and rebellion of which we human beings are guilty. He died carrying the load of the world's sin on himself. The sting of death is sin, but the sinless Jesus Christ allowed himself to be fatally stung by the wrong of us all.

The supreme act of foolishness is to spend our days on earth rejecting or neglecting God. The greatest act of wisdom is to get right with the God who made us and before whom we will all ultimately stand for our final judgment. Ask Jesus Christ right now to be your Savior and Lord in life, death, and on into eternity.

8

The Mystery of Christmas

> Then the angel said to them, "Do not be afraid, for behold, I bring you good tidings of great joy which will be to all people" (Luke 2:10).

On May 13, 1940, Sir Winston Churchill described the actions of Communist Russia as a "riddle, wrapped in a mystery, inside an enigma." Many miss the joy of Christmas and/or the gospel message because they view these phenomena as Churchill saw the U.S.S.R.—incomprehensible. However, if we could understand all God's mysteries, we would not be human, and God would not be our Holy God! The Creator is above human comprehension. He is beyond human logic but never violates it. Read again his marvelous revelation:

> In the beginning was the Word, and the Word was with God, and the Word was God. He was in the beginning with God. All things were made through Him, and without Him nothing was made that was made. In Him was life, and the life was the light of men. And the light shines in the darkness, and the darkness did not comprehend it.
>
> There was a man sent from God, whose name was John. This man came for a witness, to bear witness of the Light,

that all through him might believe. He was not that Light, but was sent to bear witness of that Light. That was the true Light which gives light to every man who comes into the world. He was in the world, and the world was made through Him, and the world did not know Him. He came to His own, and His own did not receive Him. But as many as received Him, to them He gave the right to become children of God, even to those who believe in His name: who were born, not of blood, nor of the will of the flesh, nor of the will of man, but of God.

And the Word became flesh and dwelt among us, and we beheld His glory, the glory as of the only begotten of the Father, full of grace and truth (John 1:1–14).

Christmas is a time of joy and goodwill and delighting in the age-old story of Jesus. For many, however, it just doesn't seem to make sense or fit reality. Let us look at some of the mysteries of that first Christmas.

1. *A virgin gave birth.* Seven hundred years before Christ was born, the prophet Isaiah foretold: "Therefore the Lord Himself will give you a sign: Behold, the virgin shall conceive and bear a Son, and shall call His name Immanuel" (Isa. 7:14). God chose that which was beyond human possibility to signify the coming into the world of the promised Messiah. He simply shortcut the normal, natural way of bringing children into the world, because this baby was more than a mere man. Jesus was born both of a human and of God.

2. *God became a man.* When the mayor of Chicago spent a day dressed as a tramp and living with vagrants, the Chicago Tribune described the event as "the world's greatest stoop!" The editors were wrong! Long ago, the Holy God condescended to live in this world as a man. God had every right and reason to wash his hands of the world. Instead, he loved it, especially the people who lived there. He left the wonders of heaven to come to the woes of the world. What a stoop! God was big enough to become small, and strong enough to become weak as a tiny baby.

The infiniteseminally small fetus miraculously implanted

in the womb of Mary nine months earlier was Almighty God coming to the world in the person of Jesus Christ. God became a man. Deity became as lowly dust. The Creator became like us, his creation. Jesus was fully human (with a body, feelings, and emotions). Yet the incarnate Christ was fully God, absolutely sinless, having all power, and knowing all things.

Some time ago I heard on the radio the story of a mail carrier whose wife had been killed in a car accident a couple of months before. He was sorting through lost mail at the local post office to redirect whatever parcels and letters he could. The postman opened one letter addressed to "Santa Claus" and noticed that the address at the top of the letter was his own. Looking to the bottom of the letter, he saw his only daughter's signature. The letter read:

> Dear Santa: My mommy died two months ago, and since then my daddy has been crying each night. He says only eternity will heal him. Please send a little bit of eternity to Dad this Christmas.

God has sent to all of us not only "a little bit of eternity," but the very heart of heaven. The Bible says, ". . . the Father has sent the Son as Savior of the world" (1 John 4:14). The greatest Giver sent the greatest Gift to people who had rebelled against him. It is a major theme of the Bible that Jesus is God and that he alone can rescue us from all that is wrong in the world. In the Old Testament we read, "For unto us a Child is born, unto us a Son is given; and the government will be upon His shoulder. And His name will be called Wonderful, Counselor, Mighty God, Everlasting Father, Prince of Peace" (Isa. 9:6).

John's Gospel says, "In the beginning was the Word, and the Word was with God, and the Word was God. . . . And the Word became flesh and dwelt among us, and we beheld His glory, the glory as of the only begotten of the Father, full of grace and truth" (John 1:1, 14). Later, in the same Gospel, we read, "Therefore the Jews sought all the more to kill

Him, because He not only broke the Sabbath, but also said that God was His Father, making Himself equal with God" (John 5:18).

Christ was rightly called "Immanuel—God with us," for:

> "God was manifested in the flesh, justified in the Spirit, seen by angels, preached among the Gentiles, believed on in the world, received up in glory" (1 Tim. 3:16).

> "[We are] looking for the blessed hope and glorious appearing of our great God and Savior Jesus Christ" (Titus 2:13).

> Jesus himself said, "I am the way, the truth, and the life. No one comes to the Father except through Me" (John 14:6).

> The apostle Paul wrote, "For there is one God and Mediator between God and men, the Man Christ Jesus" (1 Tim. 2:5).

3. *Christ was born to die.* Jesus Christ is the only person who ever *chose* to be born. He is also the only person who ever chose to die (a suicide is a tragedy of someone who chooses *when,* not whether, he or she will die). Christ, who need never have died, deliberately laid down his life for us all. The God-man was born to die.

A cartoon portrayed Santa with a little boy on his knee. Santa was telling the Christmas story when the boy asked, "And how did it all end?" In the background was a picture of the cross.

Hanging on a cross, at the age of thirty-three, Jesus cried out: "It is finished," having accomplished the work he was born to do. Dying, he bore in his body the sin of us all. The greatest act that Jesus did was not to heal the sick, raise the dead, still the storm, or feed five thousand, but to die on the cross, carrying on his shoulders all our guilt and shame. To fully understand Jesus Christ, including the Christmas story, one must look beyond the crib to the cross.

The angel had said to Joseph, "Call his name Jesus, for he shall save his people from their sins." Paying the punishment for the wrong of which we are guilty, Christ died to save us.

An Italian couple recently gave birth to a son. He was born to save his older brother who needed a matching bone-marrow transplant. Both children lived. Christ was born, but he had to die to save us.

4. *Christ left heaven to come to earth, so that when we leave earth we may go to heaven.* Although Jesus Christ was destined to die, after three days he rose from the dead. Christ, born from a virgin womb, rose from a virgin tomb. He conquered the grave.

Death is not the end of our existence. The Bible teaches that there is both a heaven to be gained and a hell to be shunned. The only way to be certain of heaven is to trust Christ to forgive the sin that separates us from God and would otherwise send us to hell. Our sin would keep us from everlasting life, but Christ died that our sin might be forgiven.

In May 1987, thirty-nine American seamen were killed in the Persian Gulf when an Iraqi pilot missiled their ship, the *U.S.S. Stark.* Newspapers carried a picture of the son of one of these seamen, a shy five-year-old boy, John Kiser. He was standing with his hand on his heart as his father's coffin was loaded onto a plane to take him back to the U.S.A. His mother said, "I don't have to mourn or wear black, because I know my husband's in heaven. I am happy because I know he is better off." Later on, she and young John sent a letter and an Arabic New Testament to the pilot of the Iraqi plane, addressed: "The men who attacked the Stark, Dad's ship, in the hope that it will show that even the son and the wife do not hold any grudge and are at the same time praying for the one who took the life of our father."

In life and in death, Christ the Lord is a Savior from sin and its consequences. God wants us all to have the same certainty of eternal joy that Mrs. Kiser had about her husband. We can be sure of heaven—not because we deserve it, but because the Son came to bring us into an everlasting relationship with the Father.

5. *Millions exclude Jesus Christ from his own birthday celebration.* How strange to leave out the guest of honor! Surely Christ should not be excluded from the Christmas party. Yet it has always been the same. When Mary and Joseph arrived at Bethlehem, they were told there was no room in the inn. If they arrived today, the inn's bar would probably be crowded, the game room and restaurant packed with excitement, and the business office busy! However— then and now—as people banquet, drink, laugh, and celebrate, they often inadvertently squeeze out the person for whom the festivities are intended.

Are you doing that? Or is Christ dwelling in your home and heart *every* day? If not, then you need to trust him as Savior and Lord. Ask him to forgive you and take control of your life.

Shepherds and wise men came during that first Christmas season. You today need to do the same. The mystery of Christ's coming can work the miracle of Christian conversion for anyone who asks for that new life. These words may help you to pray right now:

> Lord Jesus, I am a sinner. Thank you for coming to earth to save such as me. Thank you for dying for me and rising from the dead. Please forgive me and become my Savior and Lord. Help me daily to live for you. Amen.

9

Perfect Love

> For God so loved the world that He gave His only begotten
> Son . . . (John 3:16).

A twenty-one-year-old man, found hanging in his bedroom, left a suicide note saying only, "No one cares." In prisons, hospitals, and nursing homes, behind closed doors or even sitting in church pews, are countless people who feel the same. The sense of loneliness and of being unloved leads to awful despair, whether felt by a jilted partner, a bereaved relative, or a friendless inmate of an institution.

The three most revolutionary words ever revealed are: *God is love.* Yet, perhaps they are so familiar that we have lost sight of the tremendous truth and help they contain. They tell us sufficient about God to draw to him every hurting heart and inquiring mind. A leading theologian was asked at his retirement dinner what was the greatest thought that had ever crossed his mind. After a short pause he quoted the opening lines of a familiar hymn: "Jesus loves me, this I know, for the Bible tells me so."

No Greater Love

Staggeringly simple, yet beyond our understanding, is the truth that God, whom "heaven and the heaven of heavens cannot contain" (1 Kings 8:27) loves us as individuals and knows every detail of every life. God weighs our motives, and his penetrating eye sees all our sinful thoughts and desires. Yet *still* he loves us!

> For this reason I bow my knees to the Father of our Lord Jesus Christ, from whom the whole family in heaven and earth is named, that He would grant you, according to the riches of His glory, to be strengthened with might through His Spirit in the inner man, that Christ may dwell in your hearts through faith; that you, being rooted and grounded in love, may be able to comprehend with all the saints what is the width and length and depth and height—to know the love of Christ which passes knowledge; that you may be filled with all the fullness of God (Eph. 3:14–19).

God's love is even greater than a mother's. I read of a woman who, in the United States in the last century, was in court when her son was found guilty of a triple murder. Although she pleaded with the judge to be merciful, he was sentenced to death. She wrote many letters to the state's governor and to the country's President, pleading for clemency, but to no avail. After her son's execution the grieving mother asked for his body, desiring to bury him, but again her wish was not granted. She died a few months later, leaving just one request in her will: to be buried next to her son on the prison grounds. Such is the persistence and forgiveness of a mother's love.

God's love goes far deeper. God's love is never exhausted. It is an everlasting love, so perfect that we can say with the psalmist: "He [God] is my refuge and my fortress . . ." (Ps. 91:2). *His love is greater, too, than an earthly father's love.* King David knew what it was to have rebellious children. One was guilty of murdering his half-brother; then of turning the hearts of the people against his father; then doing battle with his father as he attempted a coup to overthrow the latter's throne. But when news of that son's death came to David, he went to his room crying, "O my son Absalom . . . if only I had died in your place!" (2 Sam. 18:33). David, of course, was aware that he had not been the devoted father he ought to have been. God, however, is perfect. Yet despite having watched us rebel against him—he still cares for us with boundless love.

God's love is also greater than the deepest romantic love. Although there is nothing in us that God should admire, still he loves us. His love does not alter, or diminish, or fade. Even our unfaithfulness toward him does not change the depth of his love. The apostle John has reminded us that "He loved us and sent His Son to be the propitiation for our sins" (1 John 4:10).

God's love is greater than charitable love. When the hearts of nations are stirred by reports of famine and starvation in Africa, we give, and rightly so. But when the next opportunity to be self-indulgent comes, we easily forget the starving millions. God is not like that. He never forgets us. The great pattern-saint, Paul, knew this. Writing to fellow Christians, he said: "But God, who is rich in mercy, because of His great love with which He loved us, even when we were dead in trespasses, made us alive . . ." (Eph. 2:4–5).

Time and time again, as you read God's Word, the Bible, you will read of our heavenly Father's love. Look in John's Gospel and it is there in Christ's words: "For God so loved the world that He gave His only begotten Son, that whoever believes in Him should not perish but have everlasting life" (John 3:16). Thus Paul wrote of "faith in the Son of God, who loved me and gave Himself for me" (Gal. 2:20). He also said: "But God demonstrates His own love toward us, in that while we were still sinners, Christ died for us" (Rom. 5:8). Have you opened your heart to God's love in your own life?

The reality of God's infinite love is demonstrated not only in the coldness of print, but also in the warmth of God's expression to us, both now and since time began. When a nation was turning its back on God centuries ago, and a preacher was challenging the people to turn from their sin to the One who loved them, a strange series of events happened. The preacher, Hosea, had married a girl of God's choice, Gomer. They had children together, but then she walked out on him. It was not just to another man, but to other men: Gomer took to the streets and became a harlot. We don't know how long this faithlessness lasted, but eventually Hosea was told by God to take Gomer back again. As he looked for her, the trail seemed endless, but he followed every lead, wandering and dashing from city to town to village, and searching in the dives and dens of evil. People surely wondered what a preacher was doing in such places!

Eventually someone told the prophet-preacher that Gomer was in the marketplace. Hosea finally found her—dirty, disheveled, with shackles around her wrists and ankles and about to be auctioned as a slave. The husband she had deserted stood among the bidders to bid a great enough price to buy her back. She was his by right because she had married him. Now she was doubly his—he had bought her. Such was the undeserved love he had toward her!

This incident was God's way of showing to the people of Israel in that day, and to us in our day, how much *he* loved us. He was willing to forgive the sin of the nation and lovingly help her, even though she had been as unfaithful as Hosea's wife. We, too, who are God's by right because he made us, can be doubly his because Christ died to buy us back, to redeem us. So great was his love for us, his unworthy beneficiaries.

The Ultimate Sacrifice

What is your sin? Are you aware of how serious it is as far as God is concerned? God hates all that is unholy, all that separates us from him and would send us to hell. Nevertheless, out of love for a rebellious world, Christ came to die, paying this awesome price for its redemption.

In his life, Jesus identified himself with the outcasts of society: the lepers, the underdogs, the suffering, the distressed. And he made himself available to those whose lives had been wrecked by sin, as he still does today. The Bible teaches that Jesus Christ was God in human form. When

God became a man, he experienced human frailty, temptation, sorrow, and suffering—and even death.

A child was looking at a litter of puppies, hoping to purchase one. He asked the old man who was selling them if he
could buy the puppy that was lying quietly on the straw, but
the man replied that it was not for sale. The boy insisted, so
the man explained that the puppy in question was lame and
therefore was not a good choice. The boy pulled up one trous-
er leg, revealing a steel brace. "I'm lame as well," he said,
"and I think I'd understand and care for that puppy better. I
know what it feels like." So, too, did Jesus identify with
humanity's weaknesses and experience all its traumas,
though he was without sin himself.

Christ's greatest act of love was to die. It was not the nails
that kept him on the cross, nor the Roman guards, but his
perfect love for every man, woman, and child—yesterday,
today, and tomorrow. As he died on the cross, the sin and
unloveliness of all humankind was laid on his suffering
body. Peter, one of Christ's disciples, explained it this way:
"For Christ also suffered once for sins, the just for the unjust,
that He might bring us to God . . ." (1 Peter 3:8). Christ loved
us so much that he paid the price for all the wrong that was
ever thought, said, and done—the sins of evil actions and
wrong attitudes.

Do you wonder if anyone loves you? Just look at the cross!
The loving God has provided a way for you to enjoy a living,
loving, lasting relationship with himself. You can know God
and have him for an intimate friend who is even closer than
a brother. He is also your caring, heavenly Father who
wants you for his family. This comes about when you
respond to his love appropriately. He commands all people to
repent—that is, to turn from whatever is wrong and to trust
Christ as Savior.

Love and the New Creation

Like a bride or groom vowing with the words, "I will," each
person needs to come to the moment in which he or she

deliberately, in repentance and faith, accepts Jesus Christ as Master and Lord. It is then, having become a real Christian—a new creation—that one begins to experience the four-dimensional love of the Lord:

1. *The breadth of God's love.* It is as broad as humanity. Everyone is included. Do you feel you are too evil or unworthy? Christ came into the world for sinners; therefore you and I qualify.

2. *The length of God's love.* It lasts forever. If you will trust Christ as Savior and Lord, you will be brought into an everlasting relationship that will take you through life, death, and eternity. We all deserve hell, but when you respond to Christ's love by trusting him, there is a place reserved in heaven for you.

3. *The depth of God's love.* Christ, the darling of heaven, stooped down to earth and came to the cross and the tomb. However low you feel you have sunk, Christ will reach down to you. He will come to the guilty, the self-important, the backslider. Whoever you are, wherever you are, Christ will come to you, but he doesn't leave you unchanged.

4. *The height of God's love.* Christ lifts up a person. He disposes of our past, directs our present, and delivers us from fear of the future. We are reborn in Christ. As a hymnwriter put it, thereby is "Love to the loveless shown that they might lovely be."

Will you today trust Christ and take him to be your Savior, Friend, and Lord? To neglect Christ's calling or reject the salvation he brings would be to abuse his sacrificial love. The consequence of bypassing Christ is so costly! Christ loved and warned us, more than any other, about the day of judgment. The God who is altogether loving is also absolutely just, so unrepented sin must be punished eternally. If you trample under foot the Lord Jesus, putting out of mind the seriousness of your sin and neglecting the warnings of the Bible, God must punish you. How tragic, when Christ loves you so much and offers you everlasting joy.

We may not be able to understand all the happenings in the world, or all of God's dealings with individuals, but it is certain that God loves you. What will you do with such love? How will you respond to God? Will you ask Christ to forgive you and live within you? If you know that God has been speaking to you and are aware of your need for him, use this following prayer to express how you feel.

Dear Holy God, I confess that I have sinned in thought, word, and deed. I want to turn from my sin. I believe your Son Jesus died for me and rose from the dead. Please forgive me and take control of my life. I want to serve you as best I can. Thank you for hearing this prayer. I ask it in the name of Jesus Christ. Amen.

10

The Key to Life

[Jesus said:] ". . . whoever drinks of the water that I shall give him will never thirst. [It] will become in him a fountain of water springing up into everlasting life" (John 4:14).

A policeman curiously watched a drunk looking for something under a street light. He asked the man what he was looking for. "My billfold," he replied. "It slipped through a hole in my pocket." They looked together, but with no success.

"Where do you think you lost it?" inquired the policeman.

"Down that road," replied the drunk, pointing into the distance.

"Then why aren't you looking down there?"

"Because there aren't any street lights there. I'd never find it!"

Many people are searching for something but they often don't look in the right place. For instance, think of the most important search of all—trying to find God and his secret of eternal life. Have you ever wished you could find and really know God? Have you ever thought that God is seeking for you?

There was once a woman whose life was a mess. She had

had five husbands and now was living with another man. Yet Jesus met and talked with her. Very lovingly he dealt with her and revealed some important truths. You can read her story in John's Gospel, chapter 4, where first we read that Jesus "needed to go through Samaria" (v. 4). Christ *wanted* to meet this woman to change her life, just as today he is willing to go out of his way to meet each of us. God cares for every individual in his creation.

Disillusioned by Life

The Samaritan woman was apparently so ashamed of her past that she went to draw water from the well at midday, when nobody would be around to see her. But Christ knew all about her. It is impossible to deceive God. No religious fanatic is good enough to impress God; no rebel is clever enough to hide anything from him.

A group of mischievous students once stuck parts of different insects together and gave the completed "bug" to a famous professor of zoology. "Can you identify this?" they asked. He studied the creature and then, looking up, said, "Yes. It's a humbug!" Neither can we deceive God—our all-knowing Creator.

In our better moments we realize we cannot even fool ourselves. Someone has reported that British entertainer Tony Hancock, who had performed before millions, committed suicide in Australia, leaving a note saying, "True happiness is impossible to obtain." The road to happiness is not paved with fun, fame, and fortune. Others find that "religion" has no reality, so they become disillusioned by the church and wonder where the real purpose in living is to be found.

Yet Christ came to offer true life. He said, ". . . I have come that they may have life, and . . . have it more abundantly" (John 10:10). Jesus sat next to a disillusioned woman and offered a new kind of life to her. He would satisfy her thirst for happiness with a fountain of joy that would never run dry.

Have you tasted this "living water" (John 4:10)?

Disappointed by Pleasure

The Samaritan woman was disillusioned by life *because* she was disappointed by pleasure. No doubt when she was a teenager, she had dreamed of her ideal husband. At last she met him, or so she thought. They married. Perhaps they were happy for a time, but slowly things turned sour. They parted and were divorced. Sadness turned to joy when she met another man. This time things looked so promising, but again her happiness was short-lived. Then there was husband number three—and four—and five. When the sixth man came along, she thought, "Why marry?" So they just lived together.

So often people have sought pleasure but found that only their pain was lasting. The actor Peter Sellers said of his life, "The realization is less than the expectation. I tell you straight, all I am trying to do is get through the day. And when I cry, I cry for yesterday."

Jesus, however, offers true pleasure, the kind that endures. To the real Christian, knowing God as a personal Friend and Savior is a pleasure beyond compare.

Distant from God

The woman at the well was disillusioned and disappointed *because* she was distant from God. She could talk about religion and the worshiping customs of her people. But a religious debate does not mean that a person has a relationship with God. Do you ever feel that God is far from you? You may not even *want* to know him—but that is a sign of your distance from him.

Do you ever wish that you could talk with God? We were made to have fellowship with God, but our wrongdoing has separated us from him. Sin is like a barrier between God and us—and we are powerless to remove it. Yet God has made the first move. He sent his Son to earth to rescue us. Christ can bring us back to God.

As Jesus talked with the Samaritan woman, she realized

that this stranger was not just an ordinary Jew or even a prophet, but that he was the promised Messiah, the Christ who had come to redeem lost mankind. *He offered her the true God:* "I who speak to you am He" (John 4:26).

Jesus has also said, "... the Son of Man has come to seek and to save that which was lost" (Luke 19:10). He came to link us up to God. Rather than being distant, God can live within a person to guide every thought, word, and deed. Life will then have meaning and purpose, whatever the future may hold.

Distorted by Sin

This woman was distant from God *because* she was marred by sin. Wrongdoing distorts every area of life, just as surely as a physical disability or illness can limit our potential in some activities. Our minds think impure thoughts. Then we tell lies and gossip or swear. We may even learn to cheat, deceive, steal. It seems so easy to do wrong but so hard to do right! Saying "nobody is perfect" does not excuse us!

The woman in John 4 was conscious of her sin, which Christ had come to deal with. She was intrigued by Jesus. After all, he had offered true pleasure, true life, and the true God. Who would not be interested? Christ had said, "But whoever drinks of the water that I shall give him will never thirst" (John 4:14a). Since she wanted that fountain of "everlasting life" she immediately replied, "Sir, give me this water." It was then that Christ touched the nerve of the problem. He said, "Go, call your husband and come here" (v. 16). Christ wanted her to admit her sin. She had to confess all to him. That would be the beginning of a new life for her.

We can never come to know God in a personal way until we admit that we have done wrong. Jesus said, "I have not come to call the righteous, but sinners, to repentance" (Luke 5:32). His greatest work was not healing the sick or even changing lives through his ministry, but dying to deal with *all* wrong. At the cross, God's anger against sin was redirected toward Christ. He became the Substitute. There our sin was laid on him, and he took the punishment we deserve. *Because he bore our sin, God can truly forgive us* and we are reconciled to him.

While on the cross, Jesus cried, "I thirst." He thirsted physically so that the spiritual thirst of all men and women could be quenched eternally. It was not easy for this woman to tell Christ about her life. It never is. But the Bible says that it is only when we confess that we are sinners who need Christ that he can and will forgive.

Not only did Christ die for us, but three days later he also triumphed over the grave. Now he desires to come and live in us, to cleanse and to control our lives. As Christ takes up residence in the hearts of those who trust him, it is as if a fountain of life springs up within, and like the woman they cannot keep it to themselves, but want to tell everyone.

Becoming a true Christian involves changing sides. It is the start of a new life. Instead of living for pleasures that so quickly pass away, you start to live for Christ, according to God's purposes. It is never easy to be a true believer in a hostile world. But Christ gives the joy and peace that come from knowing that sin is forgiven, for then the power of his risen presence enables you to overcome difficulties. True life and purpose come from having a relationship with God that lasts—through life, through death, and forever. And Jesus Christ is the key.

Are you ready to ask Christ to forgive you, to give you a new start with him by your side?

11

The Kiss of Death

[Jesus said:] "Did I not choose you, the twelve, and one of you is a devil?" (John 6:70).

If you were to visit the Florida home of Thomas Edison, you would be intrigued by a path in his garden called "The Walk of Friendship." What makes it unique is the fact that each stone was contributed by a different acquaintance of the great inventor. It is always interesting to look at the friends of famous men. But out of the whole world, Jesus Christ chose only twelve men as his closest followers. Yet it was one of those privileged few who came to be known as the most tragic figure in the Bible. That man was Judas Iscariot.

Then one of the twelve, called Judas Iscariot, went to the chief priests and said, "What are you willing to give me if I deliver Him [Jesus] to you?" And they counted out to him thirty pieces of silver. So from that time he sought opportunity to betray Him.

Now on the first day of the Feast of the Unleavened Bread the disciples. . . . did as Jesus had directed them; and they prepared the Passover. Now when evening had come, He sat down with the twelve. Now as they were eating, He said, "Assuredly, I say to you, one of you will betray Me." And they were exceedingly sorrowful, and each of them began to say to Him, "Lord, is it I?" Then He answered and said, "He who dipped his hand with Me in the dish will betray Me. The Son of Man goes as it is written of Him, but woe to that man by whom the Son of Man is betrayed! It would have been good for that man if he had not been born." Then Judas, who was betraying Him, answered and said, "Rabbi, is it I?" He said to him, "You have said it" (Matt. 26:14–17, 19–25).

[Later, in the Garden of Gethsemane:] And while He was still speaking, behold, Judas, one of the twelve, with a great multitude with swords and clubs, came from the chief priests and elders of the people. Now His betrayer had given them a sign, saying, "Whoever I kiss, He is the One; seize Him." Then immediately he went up to Jesus and said, "Greetings, Rabbi!" and kissed Him. And Jesus said to him, "Friend, why have you come?" Then they came and laid hands on Jesus and took Him. . . . Then all the disciples forsook Him and fled (Matt. 26:47–50, 56b).

As I preach in different places or get into conversation with people, I am convinced that multitudes are just like Judas. They have come so close to Christ, and yet there they stop.

A Fortunate Man

The story of Judas, as we know it, begins where the public life of Jesus began. Jesus spent time in prayer before choosing the Twelve. These men were going to be with him for the next three years while he went about his work on earth. Among them was Judas Iscariot, who is repeatedly described as "one of the twelve." As such:

1. *He heard the teaching of Christ.* Judas heard the magnificent Sermon on the Mount and parables like "The Good Samaritan," "The Prodigal Son," and "The Lost Sheep" as they first fell from Jesus' lips. He was there all along, listening to Christ's staggeringly simple, yet profound teaching. Judas would also have been by the roadside when the group of disciples sat down and Christ opened up the Scriptures to

them. For three years Judas was one of those fortunate men, listening to the words of Jesus Christ. Yet he never fully believed. He never came to a personal, intimate understanding of who Christ was, nor did he truly trust in Christ's mysterious promises.

How many people have heard all the teachings of Christ? Have you? Perhaps from childhood you were taught the Scriptures, as your mother shared Bible stories with you. Perhaps you went to Sunday school. Perhaps a Christian teacher or a friend has shared the good news about Jesus Christ with you. It is even possible that you have preached about Jesus Christ, knowing deep down in your heart that you have never responded to him personally. That was just what Judas failed to do.

2. *He saw the miracles of Christ.* Judas was once in a boat with Jesus and the other disciples, on the Sea of Galilee, when suddenly a storm arose. All the disciples panicked. They woke Jesus and cried, "Do you not care that we perish?" He stood up and said, "Peace, be still," and immediately tranquility and calm were brought to that sea. Judas saw that Jesus Christ had power over nature.

Judas was there, too, when Christ took five loaves and two fish, broke them, and fed thousands of people. Judas saw the Lord Jesus Christ heal the blind, the deaf, the lame, cleanse the lepers, and bring the dead back to life. Time after time Judas watched these miraculous events, and yet he never allowed himself to experience the miracle of Jesus Christ changing his own heart.

Perhaps you have seen miracles. You may have prayed for God to help in a time of sickness or trouble and felt God intervene. You have seen the miracles, and you know that God answers prayer. But have you ever come to him and said, "O God, do a miracle in my heart"?

3. *He saw people converted to Christ.* As one of the Twelve, Judas was with Jesus Christ when a certain devout man came to him by night. When the man left Jesus, he was not merely "religious" but right with God. And Judas came with the other disciples and joined Jesus as he sat by the well and

talked to an immoral woman. This woman was so changed by the encounter that she went back into her town and told everybody, "Come, see a man who told me all that I ever did." Some time later in that town many "believed" Jesus Christ, at least partly because of that woman's transformed life (*see* John 4).

On another occasion, Judas saw Zaccheus, a greedy tax collector, climb down from a tree. He watched Christ and Zaccheus go off together to Zaccheus's home. He saw Zaccheus come out completely changed, saying, "Have I stolen? I will repay fourfold, and half my goods I will give to the poor" (*see* Luke 19:1–10).

Judas saw people who were once utterly mixed up and torn apart by the devil's temptations come to worship the Lord Jesus Christ with perfect serenity, peace, and devotion. Judas saw many people converted, but he never experienced conversion himself.

Perhaps you, too, have seen people converted. You may know some whose language had been vile. Suddenly they were different. Their speech betrayed the change brought about when they trusted Jesus Christ. Or maybe it was a pious man who went regularly to church and worshiped God. When, suddenly, Christ himself became real to him, you realized there was something radically new. You asked him about it, and he said, "I've become right with God." If you have seen such a conversion, you know it happens. Yet perhaps it has never happened to you. A woman who had gone to church all her life once told me, "The *real* Christians have something more." That is how Judas must have felt.

4. *He did the work of Christ.* As one of the Twelve, Judas participated in the work of God and in spreading the words of Jesus. For instance, there was the time when the Lord Jesus Christ gathered seventy disciples together. He divided them up into twos and sent them everywhere to preach about God's kingdom. How thrilled they were when they came back, saying, "People have been converted. Even the devils were subject to us!" (*see* Luke 10:1–17). Judas was one

of those who gloried in all that had been accomplished, but he rejected the work of God in his own life.

Perhaps you are seeking to serve God. You may be a Sunday school teacher, or an usher at the church door. You may be an elder, or even a preacher, but that does not mean that you are right with God. In 1735, John Wesley set out as a missionary to Georgia, then a colony in America. After two years of work there, he said: "I went out to convert the Indians, but, O God, who shall convert me?" To be deeply involved in church work and noted as "a religious person," does not necessarily mean that you have peace with God. Judas participated in the work of God, and yet he never came to trust Christ as his *personal* Savior.

A Fatal Flaw

How was it, then, that Judas, the man who at first just did not "believe," eventually betrayed Jesus Christ? Something so paralyzed his conscience and his heart that he could sell, for a meager thirty pieces of silver, the God-man he had been with for so long. He secretly drifted away from Christ. Bishop J. C. Ryle said: "Open sin has killed its thousands, but secret sin its tens of thousands." That was true of Judas. He didn't suddenly say, "I'm in this for the money." It was a gradual development—and greed usually works that way.

The twelve disciples needed a treasurer. They appointed Judas. The same passage in John's Gospel that tells us that Judas was the treasurer also tells us that he was a thief from the very beginning (John 12:4–6). No doubt it started in a very small way, and perhaps at first he thought he would "borrow" only a coin or two. Then his stealing became regular. Jesus knew, of course, that Judas was beginning to sell his own soul for the love of money.

On one occasion, Mary (sister of Lazarus) came to Jesus with an alabaster box containing expensive ointment. She wanted to express her adoration for Christ, so she broke the alabaster box, poured the ointment on his feet, and washed them with her hair. The disciples began to grumble, saying: "We could have sold that and given the money to the poor." Judas was the chief one to complain. Yet it was not because he loved the poor, but because he loved money. That greed was beginning to eat away at him. Like a cancer, it was secretly, silently devouring him.

Later, when the chief priests and scribes were plotting against the Lord Jesus Christ, so they could arrest him quietly without risking any trouble from the people, they knew who would help. They made a proposal to Judas: "You betray Christ, and we'll give you thirty pieces of silver." He jumped at the opportunity. The way we receive money, and the way we spend it, not only molds us, but it also manifests what we are really like. The love of material things can distract you so much that you will not dare to trust Jesus Christ, who said: ". . . whoever of you does not forsake all that he has cannot be My disciple" (Luke 14:33).

Judas's sin was that he preferred something else to Jesus Christ. For him, it was money in hand. For you, it may be something quite different. There may be a particular pleasure, legitimate in itself, that has a grip on your life. Pleasure passes so quickly; yet to keep it, we may "trade off" Jesus Christ, the Lord of all glory.

There may be one sin that you will not let go, but you cannot enjoy it forever! Life quickly goes, and that sin can rob you of a glorious eternity with Jesus Christ. Or perhaps you may just wish to remain "respectable." Because you want to be thought well of by the people around you, are you putting off trusting the Lord for another time? One small thing, a preference for something else to Jesus, could cause you to lose your eternal bliss with God and your relationship with Christ now. Likewise, for a mere thirty pieces of silver, Judas sold Jesus Christ and lost his own soul.

A Foolhardy Plot

Christ gathered with his disciples in the upper room. He broke bread and he taught them: "Take and eat, and do it in remembrance of the fact that my body is to be broken for you." He took the cup and said, "Take and drink. It will remind you that my precious blood is going to be shed for you, that your sins might be forgiven." He went round the Twelve, including Judas, and washed their feet. Then he said, "There is one here that will betray me." How must the eleven have felt? They could scarcely believe it, but they all cried with indignation, "Lord, is it I?" Even Judas, imitating the others, addressed Jesus: "Master, is it I?" (Notice that Judas did not and could not call Jesus Lord.)

Judas knew that he was deceiving the other eleven. But it is impossible to fool Christ! He knows every detail about every person. In answer to Judas's question, the Lord Jesus replied, "You have said it." Judas got up, walked across that upper room, and went down the stairs (*see* John 13:30). I can almost hear them creak, as the traitor went down into the dark abyss of an eternal night.

After the meal, Jesus went to the Garden of Gethsemane. Judas also went there to meet Jesus. Judas's sin was not a sin of momentary passion; it was deliberate. He knew exactly what he was going to do. The Lord knew all about Judas. Nevertheless Jesus went to meet his betrayer. Judas walked up to Jesus and kissed him. He kissed the One who is the very door to heaven, but Judas would never enter that door. The Lord Jesus said to Judas, "Friend, why have you come?" What compassion Jesus had! It was as if he gave him one last opportunity to repent, but Judas refused. How long will God plead with *you?*

The Finale

A motley crew of soldiers with swords and staves arrested Jesus. There was no battle, no struggle, as they marched him away. He went calmly to the cruel cross. Remember, it was not nails that held Jesus to that cross. It was love for a lost world of sinful men and women. As he died there, all the wrong of the world was laid on him, and the Christian knows that he "has washed us from our sins in His own

blood" (Rev. 1:5). Now I ask you to consider four consequences of Judas's betrayal:

1. *He lost the promises of Christ.* We read in John's Gospel
that after Judas left that upper room and walked out into
the dark night, Christ continued to speak to his disciples.
Among other things, he said, "Let not your heart be troubled; you believe in God, believe also in Me. In My Father's
house are many mansions; if it were not so, I would have told
you. I go to prepare a place for you" (John 14:1–2). Jesus said
to the eleven disciples, "I go to prepare *a place* for you." But
Judas never heard those words. The promise was not for
him. In fact, later we find that Judas went to "his own place"
(Acts 1:25). He lost the promises of Jesus Christ.

I have often asked people a simple question: "If you were
to die tonight, would you be certain of going to heaven?"
They usually answer, "I hope so. I've never done anybody
any harm." But Jesus *promised* everlasting life. He gave the
guarantee. Stake your eternity on it! Are you certain of going
to heaven? There is no more important question.

2. *He joined the opposers of Christ.* For three years Judas
had been with Jesus. People probably laughed and mocking-
ly said, "Get back to your job. You're losing your promotion
prospects. Get back, man! Don't follow this outlaw." His family might have pleaded, but he stayed with Christ for three
whole years. At the end, he went to the chief priests and took
the money.

No sooner had Judas betrayed Jesus Christ than remorse
and regret flooded over his mind. He went back to those chief
priests and scribes and said, "I have betrayed innocent
blood. Please, get me out of this situation." "What is that to
us?" they replied. "It's your responsibility." Judas was so desperate that he took the thirty pieces of silver and threw them
on the floor of the temple in utter desperation (*see* Matt.
27:3–5).

I remember a young woman who knew she ought to trust
Jesus Christ. She had a non-Christian boyfriend who was
not interested in "spiritual things." She knew that if Christ
was to be hers, it was a special relationship—and she ought

not to date a non-Christian. She had a choice: Christ or the boy. She chose the boy and thereby joined the opposers. But not for long. Within three months the boy jilted her and she was left alone. You may ask, "Did she then become a true Christian?" No, for her heart was no longer inclined toward God. She had had her moment. God gave her a chance and she said, "No!" Have you done that? Jesus asks, "What shall it profit a man if he gain the whole world and lose his own soul?" Judas lost the promises of Christ—and he joined the opposition.

3. *He died without Christ.* I can scarcely understand how a man or woman can live without God, but I will never fathom how a person dare die without God! Judas sold God's Son for thirty pieces of silver and he didn't even have thirty days in which to spend it. What a fool! We might well wonder whether Judas really understood who Jesus Christ was or why he had come. In the Garden he said, "The one I kiss, he's the one. *Hold him fast."* Jesus could have called on twelve legions of angels, could simply have spoken the word and all his enemies would have been as dead men. Yet Judas said, "Hold him fast." Jesus is God, so how can man seize and hold him? But Christ did not need holding! He came into the world for that particular moment, with the express mission of going to the cross. He had set his face steadfastly toward Jerusalem because he knew he had to die a death whereby he would atone for the sins of the world. Even if no man had held him, he would still have gone to that cross.

The Bible tells us how Judas died: he hanged himself (Matt. 27:5). There are clues to some details. It is implied that in a potter's field, where they dug down deep for clay (and later to bury foreigners, v. 7), he hung himself over where they had been digging. Suspended between heaven and hell, Judas was wanted by neither. Eventually the branch or rope broke, and he fell headlong to the bottom, where he died. (*See* Acts 1:18–19.) Judas died without God.

There is no reason why *anyone* should die without God. When Jesus was on the cross, as God took the sin of the world and laid it on his Son, it was as if his outstretched arms were like a funnel. Now God could pour into him the sin of the world, and Christ could pay the price of it. Christ died as a substitute for sinful man.

He also died to conquer death. "My God, My God, why have You forsaken Me?" he cried (Matt. 27:46). *He* was forsaken so that we might be forgiven and never forsaken by God. We can enjoy God's presence in life, in death, and in eternity. No one need live nor die without God. Though our sins have cut us off from God, if we turn from our sins to Jesus Christ and ask for forgiveness, God will come and live within us. He will be ours, and we will be his, for all eternity. Judas, however, turned his back on Christ, and died without God.

4. *The Bible says that Judas died without hope of a heavenly home.* This is the worst consequence of all. Judas is the only man in the whole Bible who is individually named as being in hell. Christ warned about hell several times (e.g., Matt. 5:22; 23:33; Luke 12:5). After Judas died, he took the scorn of the priests who had gotten what they wanted out of him (Matt. 27:3–8). He took the scorn of the disciples when Peter stood up and said, "This man was numbered with us, but he was a traitor" (*see* Acts 1:17–18). He takes the scorn of Scripture, for being the man who betrayed Jesus Christ. And, for twenty centuries, he has taken the scorn of a world that uses his name as a contemptuous term to taunt anyone who is deceitful.

Most tragic of all is that Judas, in hell, pours scorn on *himself.* Surely he must cry out, "I was one of the Twelve. I heard the sermons, I heard the teaching, I saw the miracles, I saw people converted, I participated in the work of God." Let hell try to silence him. He will never be silenced! He is a man who was so close to Christ, but so far from him, too.

Are you like that? Close to Christ, but cut off from him because you will not come in submission and pray, "God, be merciful to me, a sinner"? Each of us has a choice: we either follow Jesus to heaven or Judas to hell. Which way will you go?

12

The Verdict Is Yours

> Pilate said to them, "What then shall I do with Jesus who is called Christ?" They all said to him, "Let Him be crucified!" (Matt. 27:22).

What a moment in time, when Christ stood on a balcony overlooking a great gathering of people from all the races of the world! Jesus was standing as the accused. Next to him was his judge, Pontius Pilate. The crowds were to be the jury. The deafening roar of excited people suddenly faded to silence when the judge asked for their verdict. What was their emphatic answer? "Crucify him, crucify him!" For many, that answer determined their eternity.

Over three years' time, thousands had lived in the wake of blessings from the work of Jesus Christ. When he raised the dead, whole families had benefited. When he healed a leper, both families and communities were helped. After the occasion when five thousand had listened to Christ for days, they went back home joyfully to share Jesus' teaching—and whole towns were uplifted. The conversion of the woman of Samaria brought the good news to an entire province.

Sadly, though, there was a growing hostility to the person of Jesus Christ. He had broken the man-made rules of the Jewish tradition; he claimed to be equal with God; he forgave people their sin; he was creating a large following, which stirred up anger and jealousy among the religious leaders of the day. Eventually, of course, he was arrested and tried several times before being sentenced to death.

Christ's Judge and Jury

Each judge and jury member knew what the right verdict for Jesus was, but they condemned him anyway. They made a decision they knew was wrong. The Bible teaches that one day every person will be judged by an all-loving and just God. Basically, all of us will be put on trial concerning our verdict on Jesus Christ. The Lord will be the judge of how we have judged him. Therefore, it is vitally important to make the right evaluation of Christ and act accordingly toward him and toward our fellowman. Those who long ago condemned Jesus did so because of selfish motives. Let us examine some of those who were involved in Christ's crucifixion. It may be that, in fact, we are looking at ourselves:

1. *Caiaphas would not leave his "religion."* Caiaphas was the distinguished high priest for the Jews, so it was before him that Christ was brought very early after his arrest. False accusations were made about Jesus, who was thereupon spat at, beaten, and struck. Though Jesus was accused of blasphemy, the religious leaders were well aware that he had performed miracles and had transformed many lives. All Christ's words and works consistently proved that he was God, come in the flesh to earth. Why did they not believe him?

Caiaphas sat in Moses' seat of honor. He knew and enjoyed religious ceremony and regalia and reveled in the quietness, mystique and tranquility of a pious atmosphere. Religious music and motifs can combine to create a unique stillness of mind and soul that is inimitable. Caiaphas knew and experienced this more than most. The thought of all this being upturned and replaced by the person and workings of Jesus Christ was more than such a religious leader could bear.

An irate Caiaphas challenged Christ: I adjure You by the

living God that You tell us if You are the Christ, the Son of God" (Matt. 26:63). When Jesus said to him, "It is as you said. Nevertheless, I say to you, hereafter you will see the Son of Man sitting at the right hand of the Power, and coming on the clouds of heaven" (v. 64), the high priest tore his clothes and accused Jesus of blasphemy. The religious hierarchy had already decided that Christ deserved death, so they began to spit on his face and hit and mock him.

It is possible to have "religion" without substance. It is possible to be "religious" without having a relationship with God and his righteousness. Are you like that? Do you really know and want him in your life? Or are you adhering only to a man-made religious system? Your verdict on the person of Christ is of infinitely more consequence than your dedication to a formal show of worship. It is even possible to be a church leader but be lost to God.

The religious people of Jesus' day were often the subject of criticism from him. In the end, it was not the drunkards, or immoral or dishonest people who crucified Christ, but their religious leaders who felt self-sufficient and therefore that they did not need Jesus. It was the common people who heard Jesus gladly. You can never rely on yourself and your deeds alone to settle eternal matters. There must be a moment of turnaround, a realization that one must trust in Christ alone to save. Jesus said, ". . . unless you are converted and become as little children, you will by no means enter the kingdom of heaven" (Matt. 18:3). That applies even to the most "religious." Beware of a Christ-less religion. Jesus reminded us that on the day of judgment there will be many who say, "Lord, Lord, have we not prophesied in Your name, cast out demons in Your name, and done many wonders in Your name?" (see Matt. 7:22). But Christ will declare, "I never knew you, depart from Me, you who practice lawlessness!" (v. 23).

Paul wrote: "For there is one God and one Mediator between God and men, the Man Christ Jesus" (1 Tim. 2:5). Peter preached, "Nor is there salvation in any other, for there is no other name under heaven given among men by which we must be saved" (Acts 4:12). Jesus himself said, "I am the way, the truth, and the life. No one comes to the Father except through Me" (John 14:6). Have you "religion," or Christ? Those who hold to ceremonial piety and pomp often let go of Jesus Christ.

2. *Pilate would not leave his neutrality.* The Bible says, "When morning came, all the chief priests and elders of the people took counsel against Jesus to put Him to death. And when they had bound Him, they led Him away and delivered Him to Pontius Pilate the governor" (Matt. 27:1–2). The Jewish religious leaders, not legally allowed to sentence Christ to death, passed him on to Pilate, who could. The Roman governor, they hoped, would try Jesus and have him executed. Pilate knew that Christ was innocent, but he refused to leave his neutral position.

Politics were at work here. Pilate had been governor of the province since A.D. 26. He was in charge of the occupying army and of the tax system and had the power to appoint the high priest. He also was authorized to sentence any subject to death. As procurator of restless Judea, Pilate had already known trouble. He had set up images of the emperor in Jerusalem, the Holy City of the Jews, whom he thus antagonized. The resentment this caused eventually led to a confrontation and slaughter of a large number of Jews. As a weak man, Pilate was now desperate to pacify the Jews. He wanted to appear to be their friend and was willing to keep the peace at any cost, even if that meant going against his own principles of fairness.

In Pilate's view, Christ was not guilty of any crime. Twice Pilate had cross-examined Jesus (*see* Luke 23:1–4, 13–25), finally turning to the crowds and asking, "What evil has he done?" Pilate's wife even sent a message to her husband, saying, "Have nothing to do with that just Man, for I have suffered many things today in a dream because of Him" (Matt. 27:19). Anxious to wriggle out of a troublesome dilemma, Pilate used a custom of the day, namely to release a prisoner at that time of feasting. So he asked the crowd to choose for him. Should he release a notable rioter and murderer named Barabbas—or Jesus, the miracle worker? When the mob, swayed by self-serving religious leaders, chose freedom for Barabbas, Pilate both literally and figuratively washed his hands of all that was to happen.

Did Pilate really believe that cleansing himself of responsibility, by having the crowd decide who was to die, would excuse his part in the trial and sentencing? The world has decided differently. Every minute, somewhere in the world, a congregation repeats the words of the creed, saying that Christ "suffered under Pontius Pilate." This spineless weakling tried to juggle to please the crowds, the religious authorities, his wife, Rome, and his own twisted conscience. He should have listened more closely to Christ, whose words and works had shown that it is impossible to please both God and man. People who hope only to please others will never please God. Pressure from the crowd, "fear of men" (as Jesus called it), can rob a person of fellowship with God. You are either against Christ or for him. It is impossible to be neutral, to "straddle the fence."

History tells us that Pilate lost the favor of Rome and ended his days as a demented outcast. Even if he had succeeded in his career and won the approval of the Jews, it would have been of little value because God was his enemy. When a person follows Christ, it has to be an unreserved taking up of the cross, denying self, and walking in his footsteps. If the world hated Jesus, they will do the same to his followers. However, whatever the cost as far as the present is concerned, Christ promises his presence as the Friend who is totally faithful and beside every believer forever. That is a more valuable relationship than anything the world can offer.

3. *Herod would not leave his sin.* When, after his first interrogation, Pilate sent Jesus to Herod (Luke 23:6–7), it would have been surprising if there had been a fair trial. Herod Antipas had already proved his preference for sin rather than truth (*see* ch. 4: "Sin's Progression"). He came from a family renowned for its evil. His father, Herod the Great, had ordered the death of all baby boys under the age

of two in Bethlehem at the time of Jesus' birth, in the hope of destroying the rumored "king of the Jews." He himself, after divorcing his wife to marry the wife of his half-brother Philip, had been accused of immorality by John the Baptist. Eventually this weak and wicked man had followed the whim of his ill-gotten wife and had John executed. In silencing the voice of the Baptist, he believed he had silenced the voice of God.

Stories and reports of all that Jesus had done reached Herod's palace—the blind seeing, the deaf hearing, the dumb speaking, the lame walking, the leper being cleansed, and the dead raised. The news made Herod wonder. When his conscience was alert, he even wondered if John the Baptist had come back to life! While Herod was in Jerusalem to celebrate the Passover, suddenly his officials came with the news that Pilate had sent the miracle worker to him. Herod was delighted, for now he could find out more about the man of whom he had heard so much. Perhaps he could be entertained by some miracle?

Like a child full of excitement, he asked Christ to perform a sign, a wonder. However, since it is only the devil who works the spectacular to get a following, Jesus remained silent. If Herod could callously cut off the voice of John the Baptist, who spoke as "thus saith the Lord," why should Jesus say anything further? The silence of God can be as awesome as his voice! Within minutes, Herod's emotion was transformed from one of eager excitement to absolute anger and rage. Losing his patience and self-control, Herod treated Christ with contempt and mocked him before sending him back to Pilate once again.

Have you ever thought that atheists and skeptics are basically dishonest people? The Book of Romans, chapter one, makes it clear that the real cause of disbelief is an unwillingness to leave sinful and selfish living. It is not that people cannot believe, but rather that they will not. Those who trust Christ must be willing to leave and renounce sin as they come to the Savior of sinners.

4. *Individuals would not leave the crowd.* Although those

were cruel and brutal days, and people would find their
entertainment in watching folk being executed, surely there
was a sense of justice and fair play in some. Yet multitudes
thronged to watch the spectacle of Jesus of Nazareth's trial
by Pilate. It was clear to them that Pilate was waiting for a
chance to free Jesus Christ, but here was their opportunity
to manipulate a despised Roman authority as well as curry
favor with their religious leaders. Instead of calling for
Jesus' release, the whisper went around to call for Christ's
blood. "Crucify him!" they shouted. Not a single, lone voice
had the courage to cry out in Jesus' defense and defy the
mainstream. Was there not a blind man in the crowd to
whom Jesus had given sight? Were no cleansed lepers there?
Were there none of the five thousand whom Jesus had fed in
the thronging multitude? It seemed that all the people
joined in one mass to cry out against Jesus—or held back
their objections out of fear. Christian conversion involves a
willingness to turn one's back on sin, including "the crowds"
who embrace wrongdoing. It means swimming against the
tide. It involves standing against the trends of the day and
speaking up for Christ and his Word. That is not easy, but if
we ask him Christ will give his strength to do what is right.

It seems that all of humanity was represented that tragic
day in wrongly judging Jesus. Caiaphas was a Jew, Pilate a
Roman, Herod an Edomite, and the crowds were both Jew
and Gentile. But today the verdict is yours. Imagine yourself
in that multitude, standing with all those people. You are
asked the age-old question, "What shall we do with Jesus
Christ?" Will you merely give the age-old answer, "Away
with him"?

Everybody is confronted with the decision to turn either
toward Jesus or away from him, to receive or reject him, to
believe in him or to doubt God's Word. When the crowd
shouted, "His blood be on us and on our children," they were
uttering some of the saddest words in all the Bible. It is a
fearful thing to reject Christ and fall into the hands of the
living God on the inevitable day of judgment.

A Vital Decision

You are part of that jury, too, but this time it is your own future at stake. The verdict is yours. What will *you* do with Jesus Christ? You need him . . .

In Life

Life is both haphazard and dangerous without Jesus Christ. All humanity was made to know God. It is sin that separates us from our Creator. We need Christ in life to forgive past transgressions and give us power over potential sin in the future. Sin is a gripping and deadly attraction for all of us.

There was once an eagle who swooped down onto a floating ice block to pick at the flesh of an animal carcass lying there. Little did the bird know that the block was headed toward a huge waterfall. The block moved faster and faster. Finally, as it began to tumble over the falls, the bird realized the danger and spread its wings to fly away, as it had done so many times before. This time, though, the eagle had remained too long in a dangerous situation—and its claws had become imbedded in the ice. Instead of soaring upward, it fell to a watery death, squawking as it went into the abyss.

Sin is like that. It gradually puts a grip on us until it finally drags us down into destruction. We need Christ to deliver us from past sin, present temptation, and evil enticements in the future.

In Death

Who knows when the curtain will finally close on your life! The tree from which your coffin will be constructed may already have been felled. Verna Wright, professor of rheumatology at Leeds University, was once asked on television, "What does Christianity offer which nothing else offers?" The reply was "Comfort for a dying man."

If you accept Christ as your Savior and Lord, he promises his presence, even as you walk through the valley of the shadow of death. Patricia St. John tells a story that illustrates why this is so. A family was picnicking when the peace was disturbed by a bee hovering over the little girl. She screamed and panicked, though her father tried to assure her that the bee would fly away if she simply remained still. However, she was still fearful and continued to jump around. Eventually the father stood to swipe the bee away. As he did, it stung him, then shook itself free and flew away. The father turned to the girl and removed her fear by saying, "A bee can only sting once—and *I* have taken the sting."

The sting of death, says the Bible, is sin. Our knowledge of wrongdoing creates our fear of the unknown future. Christ, though, out of love has taken the sting of sin and death itself. As he hung on the cross, all our sin was transferred to Christ. He bore it in his own body, so that if we repent and believe, he will grant us his abiding presence in life and in death.

In Eternity

Christ not only died; he also rose from the grave. At Easter time 1988, British stamps were franked by the post office with the words "Jesus Is Alive." That is absolutely true, and it is a first-class message! There is life after death, and both heaven and hell are taught in the Bible. It is so important to make sure of a place reserved in heaven for you. Christ died to remove the sin that otherwise would keep you from heaven. Eternity depends on what you will do with Jesus Christ. Will you acknowledge him as your Master? The verdict is yours. What will you do with Jesus Christ? One day you will be wondering, "What will he do with me?"

13

Will You Meet Jesus Christ Today?

[Job said:] "For I know that my Redeemer lives, and He shall stand at last on the earth" (Job 19:25).

Disillusioned! Despairing! Despondent! Have you ever felt like that? Those were human emotions felt by two men walking the seven miles from Jerusalem to Emmaus almost two thousand years ago. For three years Jesus of Nazareth had been speaking, performing miracles, and changing lives. Many believed that he was the Messiah promised for Israel. Instead he had been crucified, which seemed utterly senseless to his followers. After all, Jesus had raised the dead, cast out demons, stilled the stormy waters, fed five thousand with five loaves and two fishes. Could he not, therefore, avoid crucifixion? Surely he could have foiled his enemies' evil plans!

Now behold, two of them were traveling that same day to a village called Emmaus, which was about seven miles from Jerusalem. And they talked together of all these things which had happened. So it was, while they conversed and reasoned, that Jesus Himself drew near and went with them. But their eyes were restrained, so that they did not know Him.

And He said to them, "What kind of conversation is this that you have with one another as you walk and are sad?"

Then the one whose name was Cleopas answered and said to Him, "Are You the only stranger in Jerusalem, and have You not known the things which happened there in these days?" And He said to them, "What things?" And they said to Him, "The things concerning Jesus of Nazareth, who was a Prophet mighty in deed and word before God and all the people, and how the chief priests and our rulers delivered Him to be condemned to death, and crucified Him. But we were hoping that it was He who was going to redeem Israel. Indeed, besides all this, today is the third day since these things happened. Yes, and certain women of our company, who arrived at the tomb early, astonished us. When they did not find His body, they came saying that they had also seen a vision of angels who said He was alive. And certain of those who were with us went to the tomb and found it just as the women had said; but Him they did not see."

Then He said to them, "O foolish ones, and slow of heart to believe in all that the prophets have spoken! Ought not the Christ to have suffered these things and to enter into His glory?" And beginning at Moses and all the Prophets, He expounded to them in all the Scriptures the things concerning Himself.

Then they drew near to the village where they were going, and He indicated that He would have gone farther. But they constrained Him, saying, "Abide with us, for it is toward evening, and the day is far spent." And He went in to stay with them. Now it came to pass, as He sat at the table with them, that He took bread, blessed and broke it, and gave it to them. Then their eyes were opened and they knew Him; and He vanished from their sight. And they said to one another, "Did not our heart burn within us while He talked with us on the road, and while He opened the Scriptures to us?" (Luke 24:13–32).

Everything this world offers is a disappointment. But Christ is not. He meets our expectations and is real in an ever-deepening way to those who know him. It did not seem like that to Cleopas and his friend because they had been making three mistakes.

First, they were *unmindful of Scripture's prophecy.* The Bible, the inspired Word of God written over a period of sixteen hundred years, is full of Jesus Christ. The Old

Testament looked forward to his coming as Messiah. Later, the New Testament affirmed his incarnation, looked forward to his second coming, and described a Christian's proper relationship with the Savior and with other people.

The Old Testament details how Christ would die for our sins (e.g., Ps. 22; Isa. 53), predicting, too, his resurrection: ". . . Nor will you allow Your Holy One to see corruption" (Ps. 16:10). Jesus had foretold, "Destroy this temple, and in three days I will raise it up" (John 2:19). On another occasion, Christ had predicted, "Behold, we are going up to Jerusalem, and the Son of Man will be betrayed to the chief priests and to the scribes; and they will condemn Him to death, and deliver Him to the Gentiles to mock and to scourge and to crucify. And the third day He will rise again" (Matt. 20:18–19).

For various reasons, Jesus' followers had not grasped what he and the Bible were saying. The truths did not penetrate their minds. Refusing to allow Bible promises to undergird their outlook, distress had overwhelmed them. The Bible gives promises that cover every eventuality of life, but often we act on the cynic's advice: "Why trust when you can worry!"

The *second* mistake made by the two men on the way to Emmaus was to *fail to understand salvation's plan.* Man's natural inclination is to try to reach God by self-effort and self-improvement. This approach never succeeds. Millions trudge along the treadmill of observing religious restrictions and ritual without resting in the good news of how God has worked to bring us to know him.

As soon as sin came into the world, God began to unfold his plan to rescue mankind from the power and penalty of rebellion against him. In the days before Christ walked on earth, animals were sacrificed as substitute for guilty persons who had sinned and deserved death. An Israelite would take a lamb or goat to the priest, and both of them would lay their hands on the head of the animal before it was killed. Although unaware of it then, they were picturing Christ who, in the fullness of time, would actually die as the Lamb of God to take away the sin of the world (*see* Lev. 4;

16:21–22). Seven hundred years before the death of Christ, Isaiah prophesied about Jesus: ". . . He was led as a lamb to the slaughter, and as a sheep before its shearers is silent, so He opened not His mouth. . . . yet it pleased the LORD to bruise Him; He has put Him to grief. . . . He shall see the travail of His soul and be satisfied . . ." (Isa. 53:7, 10–11).

The apostle Paul explains what happened when Christ died: ". . . I declare to you the gospel which I preached to you, which also you received and in which you stand, by which also you are saved. . . . For I delivered to you first of all that which I also received: that Christ died for our sins according to the Scriptures, and that He was buried, and that He rose again the third day according to the Scriptures . . ." (1 Cor. 15:1–4).

Three times Christ had spoken of his being "lifted up" to die. He said that when this happened he "will draw all peoples" to himself (John 12:32). This tells us that Christ is *the way*. He also said, "When you lift up the Son of Man, then you will know that I am He" (John 8:28). Christ is *the truth*. He told us, too, that "as Moses lifted up the serpent in the wilderness, even so must the Son of Man be lifted up, that whoever believes in Him should not perish but have eternal life" (John 3:14–15). Christ is *the life*.

When soldiers brutally treated Christ and crucified him, God was not caught unaware. Men "did their worst" against Jesus, but—in a way—so did God! Out of loving concern for us, God laid our sin on his Son. Christ carried it and paid for it all. That is the only way God has provided whereby our sin, which separates us from him, can be removed and forgiven. Christ's death reveals and satisfies God's justice, since sin was punished; it also reveals God's love and mercy, since sinners can be forgiven and reconciled to their Creator. There will be disillusionment among all who are honest enough to face their guilty conscience yet do not recognize God's salvation plan. All are powerless to clear the past or change themselves for the future. No wonder the two walking to Emmaus were so downcast!

However, there was a *third* reason for their heaviness of

heart: the two men were *unaware of the Savior's presence.* As they were walking, Jesus himself drew near, but God "restrained" their eyes so that they did not recognize the risen Lord. It would have seemed too good to be true, yet it was a fact. Jesus had bodily risen from the dead. Christ was not just a spirit on that road. As he was to say a little later to his disciples: "Behold My hands and My feet, that it is I Myself. Handle Me and see, for a spirit does not have flesh and bones as you see I have" (Luke 24:39). He who had been placed in the tomb had come out! Jesus was risen, yet the two who walked with him to Emmaus were unaware of his presence.

How did Christ deal with the threefold mistake that was postponing an end to their grief? He dealt with each misunderstanding in his own special way:

1. *Jesus opened the Scriptures.* The whole Bible testifies of Christ. Just as the English Royal Navy's rope has running throughout it a crimson cord, so also does the Bible have entwined from beginning to end the blood-red theme of Christ and his death for us. Firmly, but compassionately, Jesus spoke to his two followers and said, "O foolish ones, and slow of heart to believe in all that the prophets have spoken!" Then ". . . He expounded to them in all the Scripture the things concerning Himself." What a wonderful sermon that must have been! All the world's finest oratory could not compare with Christ's revelation of himself in Scripture. The two men testified to this: "Did not our hearts burn . . . while He opened the Scripture to us?" Jesus later said to the eleven, "These are the words which I spoke to you while I was still with you, that all things must be fulfilled which were written in the Law of Moses and the Prophets and the Psalms concerning Me" (Luke 24:44).

Jesus Christ is in all the Scriptures. Pierce the Bible in any place, and his blood will flow. Christ is concealed in the Old Testament and revealed in the New. If you find your faith faltering and difficult to maintain, turn to the Bible, asking God to instruct you, and faith will come by reading and hearing his Word. Jesus knew this, so he used the Scriptures to bless Cleopas and his friend. We do not require any *new* revelations today, because the Word of God can meet every need, as it has in the past.

2. *Jesus opened their understanding.* He dealt with their being unmindful of Scripture's prophecy by "opening the Scriptures to them" (*see* Luke 24:33). The Bible was given by God to *all* people: ". . . no prophecy of Scripture is of any private interpretation, for prophecy never came by the will of men, but holy men of God spoke as they were moved by the Holy Spirit" (2 Peter 1:20–21). To truly understand the Bible, we must listen to God speak. It is a book that is spiritually discerned, so we must hear with both clean minds and open hearts. Christian faith is given by God. The mind, which the Bible describes as being "at enmity with God," "blinded," "defiled," and "unbelieving" can be renewed: ". . . be transformed by the renewing of your mind, that you may prove what is that good and acceptable and perfect will of God" (Rom. 12:2). William Wilberforce, the Christian Member of Parliament from Yorkshire who was responsible for the abolition of slavery in England, once took William Pitt the Younger to hear the gospel preached in an Anglican Church. Pitt, a genius of a man who eventually became Prime Minister of Great Britain, listened to a straightforward, forthright sermon explaining the gospel. Walking away together afterward, Wilberforce asked Pitt what he thought of the message. Pitt replied by explaining that he could not make sense of it at all.

The gospel *is* one of God's mysteries, so intellect is not a guarantee of one's ability to grasp its spiritual truth. Yet, if God gives understanding, a little child will be able to grasp what the greatest minds cannot fathom. Ask God to instruct you. He will open your understanding. Then open the Scriptures for yourself.

3. *Jesus opened their eyes.* The two travelers to Emmaus did not understand salvation's plan so Jesus opened their understanding (*see* Luke 24:45). The hearts of the two men were ultimately cheered, of course, when they saw the Christ they knew had been crucified and whose body they feared had been stolen. The Lord Jesus promises his

ence to all those who trust him as Savior and Lord. How sad, therefore, to go through life without ever finding the Lord God as a Friend and Helper.

In Freiburg, Germany, there is a beautiful organ in a magnificent Gothic cathedral. One elderly church organist had always treated the instrument with great pride and care. While practicing one day, he was approached by a man who asked if he could play the organ for a while. A curt refusal was given. The stranger sat in the church pews and listened to the older man. Then he asked again, and later a third time. Finally the old organist slid a little along the organ bench, allowing the younger man to play. As he did, such beautiful music filled the church that the old organist was startled and asked the young man's name. "Mendelssohn," was the reply. "To think I nearly didn't allow the master to play the organ!" said the old man in adulation.

Do not miss the opportunity presented to you today, to allow the Master to cleanse you from sin and control your life—to allow him to be your Lord and Master. Open your eyes and heart. Today is the day to meet Jesus, and tomorrow may be too late.

In December 1985, early one morning, there was a multiple pile-up of cars and trucks in thick fog on the London orbital motorway. A policeman later described the horror of that morning. He told how he quickly arrived at the scene of the accident and tried to flag down vehicles speeding toward the stationary cars. None of the drivers paid any attention. Desperately he waved warning flares, but still the drivers raced on and he could hear them crashing in the fog. Tears rolled down his cheeks, he said, as he felt his powerlessness to prevent further disaster.

In like manner, writing these words, I would urge *you* to and trust Christ. Do it today, before it is rist longs to forgive you and meet your ill you acknowledge him now as your rd, and Friend? Yes, you *can* meet Jesus

14

Someone Worth Living For

> Let this mind be in you which was also in Christ Jesus,
> who, being in the form of God. . . . He humbled Himself and
> became obedient to the point of death . . . (Phil. 2:5–6, 8).

Nearly two thousand years after Christ walked on earth, he is still the center of attention. Some love him, others hate him. On radio and television, in schools, magazines, the workplace, and sports grounds, his name is taken in vain, even ridiculed and blasphemed. It is as if there is a concerted attack on this one man and all he represents.

Yet, in all of history, Jesus Christ is unique and towers above those who want to trample on him. There are five basic facts about Jesus that we all need to consider:

1. *You cannot explain Christ.* Jesus is beyond human logic or understanding. He cannot be interpreted through either scientific or philosophical explanations. Jesus Christ is the one historical personage whose life was written before he was born. Before he had set foot in the arena of human history, his biography had already been penned. I love reading biographies and autobiographies, but if I came across the life story of somebody not yet born, I would call it fiction! But the manner and place of Christ's birth; his works, teachings, and miracles—the way in which he would die, and miraculously

rise from the dead—all were prophesied and written down long before he came into the world.

Jesus Christ was born in a manger, yet wise men from the East, following a bright star, came and worshiped him, bowing before a little baby. Others also sensed something special about that baby, and authorities on the Jewish Law later sat discussing it with him when he was just twelve years of age.

Here was a man of miracles (thirty-six are recorded in the Gospels). Only God could take five loaves and two fishes, break them and feed five thousand people, with plenty left over. No one else could speak to the deaf so that they could hear, or bring words to the lips of the dumb, and sight to blind eyes. Only Christ could say to a lame man, "Get up and walk," so that, in front of an astonished crowd, he did. Certainly Christ alone could raise from the dead a twelve-year-old girl, a young man, and an older man who had already been entombed. You cannot explain Christ! He once spoke to a fig tree, and its process of withering (which would normally have taken years) happened overnight. Jesus spoke to a storm at sea, when wind and waves were beating against his little boat. His "Peace, be still!" brought instant calm to a tempestuous sea. Christ had power over the devil and over nature, including disease and death. He even had power over his own death, saying: "No man can take my life; I have power to lay it down, and I have power to take it up again."

At every major event in the Bible, each person of the Trinity was at work. It was so when Jesus rose from the dead. The Bible teaches that God the Father raised Jesus from the dead (1 Cor. 6:14); that he was raised by the power of the Holy Spirit (Rom. 8:11); that he raised himself by his own power (John 2:18–22). Many ignore or deride Jesus, but they cannot explain either his life or his death and resurrection. Christ was sinless, pure, holy, and undefiled. He turned to his enemies and asked, "Which one of you convicts me of sin?" He looked to his Father and said: "I delight to do your will." You may criticize the church establishment and argue about doctrine. But could you explain Christ—except that he is God come down in the flesh? Scores of worldly leaders have had their moment. Now they are gone, mere names in history books. Contrast Christ's impact. He never compelled people to follow him, yet—out of love and nearly two thousand years later—millions are willing to "put off the old man" (Col. 3:9) to live for him. You cannot explain him.

2. *You cannot equal Christ.* No one but Jesus Christ has ever been able to live without sin. He never apologized or blushed with embarrassment—he did not need to. It was never necessary for Jesus to withdraw a single word or modify a single act. Everything he said and did was perfectly balanced.

He showed no sign of regret or remorse for a misused opportunity and never felt guilty. Because there was nothing for him to feel guilty about, he never experienced the pain of an accusing conscience. John, who was very close to Christ, said, "*In* Him is no sin." Peter, the man of action, said, "He *did* no sin." Paul, the great intellectual, said, "He *knew* no sin." The Book of Hebrews, which is all to do with the old and the new covenants, said, "He is *without* sin." Even his judge, Pilate, said, "I find no fault in this man." Judas Iscariot, who sold Jesus Christ for thirty pieces of silver, said: "I have betrayed innocent blood." The soldier who supervised Jesus' crucifixion said, "Surely He was the Son of God." No man can equal his purity.

Many great religious leaders have lived, died, and been buried, and that was the end of it. Millions follow Mohammed, but he is dead and buried. Millions follow Buddha, but he also is dead and buried, as are scores of spiritual gurus. But Christ rose bodily from the dead and sent his Spirit down to us. You cannot equal Christ. There is no man like him, for he is both man *and* God.

Christ was in complete control of his emotions. He did not panic when there were five thousand people to be fed, or when the lepers came to be healed. Theologian Graham Scroggie has argued that there was in Jesus' personality a perfect balance between his solemnity and his joy; between his aloofness in private prayer and his sociability at the wedding in Cana; between his dignity before Pilate and his humility and meekness; between his profundity and his simplicity (for example, in the parables); between his severity against the hypocrisy of the Pharisees and his tenderness to the woman caught in the act of adultery; between his great energy in going about doing things and his resting in his Father's presence. Jesus Christ loved God and he loved man, a perfect equilibrium! You will never equal him in any way.

3. *You cannot exclude Christ.* In some countries, the worship of God is brutally suppressed; in others it is horribly perverted and twisted. In the West, it is buried under materialism, humanism, and pleasure seeking. God, however, often acts as the "hound of heaven," pursuing relentlessly those he longs to draw to himself.

An atheist once mocked a Christian by saying: "If there is a God, let him strike me dead in the next five minutes." The Christian replied, "Do you think you can exhaust the patience of God in five minutes?" The Lord's love and compassion leads him to pursue his children patiently. You can never completely exclude Christ from your life. The heart of God urges his people to turn from their sins and return to him. Christ stood over Jerusalem and groaned: "O Jerusalem. . . . How often I wanted to gather your children together, as a hen gathers her brood under her wings, but you were not willing!" (Luke 13:34).

It is strange that whether people are atheists or merely comedians seeking to make a living with tasteless "humor," the theme of God or eternity is never far from their lips. If these things do not exist, why are we fascinated with them? Eternity has been so imprinted in our minds that whatever our morality, we still have a sense of God. Jesus Christ and the Bible's revelation are responsible for the most radical changes in the lives of millions, as well as having been the prime influence of ethics, customs, legal system, architecture, art, music, literature, and history on many cultures.

4. *You cannot escape Christ.* Those who ignore all the ardent yearnings of God toward them should hear the Bible's teaching that there is a forthcoming judgment for *all.*

Those who on earth have said to God, "Depart from me," will face him, the ultimate Judge, pronouncing the same words to them. He controls the eternal destiny of every man, woman, and child. Heaven and hell are realities that nobody can escape. How strange, though, that people should want to escape from God, who rules not as a tyrant, but as a loving heavenly Father who longs to give the best to his children. Why should anyone want to escape him, except because of unwillingness to leave one's selfish, sinful ways?

Jesus Christ is pursuing you. Why do you run away? Christ left heaven to come to earth and die for you. Today he desires that you trust him and accept his loving lordship. God sets his loving sight on all people. Who would want to escape such everlasting joy?

5. *You can experience and enjoy Christ.* Millions have found that Jesus Christ is not just a figure of history who set a moral example, or a prophet who promised a future kingdom, but the One who meets the deepest present needs. We are born to live, and Christ was born to die, so that we can live in eternity. Because Christ was sinless, death (which is the consequence of sin) had no claim on him. But out of love for us, Jesus chose to pay the price of sin for us all. Christ's life, death, and resurrection form a rescue mission.

The now-risen Jesus longs to forgive each one of us personally. When we repent and believe, the sin that separates us from God is instantly removed and we are brought into a living, loving, lasting relationship with God. Jesus wants you to experience God in your own life. He disposes of the past, enriches the present, and directs the future. This is possible only through the finished work of Christ. No matter how sinful your life may have been, Jesus is willing to cleanse you completely and abide within you.

Over two centuries ago, a wealthy landowner, Sir Roger Boulter, visited the traveling fair at Colchester. As he went round the stalls and sideshows, he suddenly heard the market-square clock begin to chime. Like a child, he count-ed, but he could not believe his ears. The clock chim
teen! He thought he had miscounted until a small d

low standing next to him turned and verified the happening by saying, "The clock struck thirteen." That night Sir Roger recorded the incident in his diary.

Two months later, Sir Roger woke up and sensed a compelling inward voice that said, "Go to York." He was not a man given to such voices, but the next day he saddled his horse and set off to York. As he arrived there was a large crowd gathered outside the courthouse. On hearing that it was the last day of a murder trial, he entered the courthouse and sat in the public gallery, from where he heard the guilty verdict pronounced. When the accused man was asked if he had anything to say, he replied: "I am innocent. I was more than one hundred miles from the crime on the day it took place. I was in Colchester. Another man and myself heard a clock strike thirteen. If only I could find him, he could vouch for my innocence." Immediately Sir Roger stood up and declared: "Now I know why I was to come to York." He explained who he was and showed the judge his diary which he always carried with him. The accused was declared innocent on the basis of Sir Roger's testimony. As he and Sir Roger walked out of the court, the freed man turned to his benefactor and said, "You are the only man in all the world who could have saved me."

That is what Christ is to you—utterly unique and absolutely vital for your salvation. He is willing and able to save you from the penalty, power, and ultimately the presence of sin. Jesus loved you enough to die for you. Surely you should trust him and live for him!

15

A Plea for Purity

Draw near to God and He will draw near to you. Cleanse your hands, you sinners; and purify your hearts, you double-minded (James 4:8).

Last year the little family was together. Mealtimes were a joy, and other shared activities were a regular occurrence. Now the family is suffering, barely making the best of what remains. The harmony and joy are gone, probably forever. Why? Because one parent has left the fold to pursue an adulterous relationship. That story is repeated thousands of times these days, but what is most disconcerting is that it is happening even in Christian homes.

The breakup of a marriage often begins with a gradual distancing between two partners with different interests and goals. There may already be a casual attraction on the part of one spouse for someone else. If not, a neighborhood social event or even a business meeting with someone of the opposite sex may provide the spark that ignites the fire of unlawful passion.

It is time that we take stock of ourselves as Christians. Do our lives reflect the purity of thought and action we are called on to display? Far too often we silently ignore the flirting, adultery, and general immorality in our ranks until we begin to distort our own standards to the brink of disaster. We are almost accustomed to hearing of yet another family shipwrecked on the rocks of immorality, having drifted there on the silent tides of compromise. Sometimes we suddenly discover that the devastated family is our own!

God's clear command "You shall not commit adultery" is generally accepted as a basic rule of living by the people of God. But we may tend to forget what that implies. God also commanded, "You shall not covet . . . anything that is your neighbor's," and elsewhere told us to "abstain from fornication," "keep yourself pure," "flee youthful lusts," and to avoid "all appearance of evil." A biblical gallery of failures in that area of behavior consistently warns us—whether it be Reuben, Judah, Samson, Eli's sons, David and his sons, or the Israelites or Corinthians in general. Despite all those case studies, the world's immorality has spilled over into the church.

The Perils of Adultery

The early chapters of the Book of Proverbs deal specifically with sexual sinning, and chapter 5 describes the folly of adultery, giving ten reasons to avoid it.

1. *It is based on deceit* (v. 3). How glamorous impurity appears at first! What rich rewards there seem to be! It all looks so easy, so sweet and smoothly acquired. Stolen waters are pleasant initially, until they turn sour and leave a trail of heartbreak. The innocent suffer, and so do the guilty. God's commands are not grievous but are for our good and blessing, although "the father of lies" will tell us otherwise.

2. *Its consequences are disastrous* (v. 4). Immorality of heart and body robs a person of joyful Christian living and zealous service. How many believers refrain from witnessing or are silent at prayer meeting because the bitterness of moral defeat is plaguing their lives? How tragic that what one generation excuses in moderation, the next will embrace in excess. No wonder so many parents find cause to grieve

over their children's open and shameless promiscuity. The children were disillusioned observers of their parents' secret compromises. It seemed inconsistent to them to love and obey a Lord who appeared to have left their parents' passions uncontrolled.

3. *Its results are damning* (v. 5). The world gleefully points a finger, taunting the church whenever it hears of an immoral pastor or wayward member. Evasive statements may come from the pulpit concerning the practical nitty-gritty of "pure living," because insisting on high standards might condemn the preacher as well! No wonder this is so, when even regular churchgoers indulge in reading immoral newspapers, listening to smutty comedians, or simply becoming flirts. As Bishop Ryle said, "We should not expect sin, nor excite sin, nor excuse sin." Just as atheism and unbelief are symptoms of unrighteousness and corruption (*see* Rom. 1:18–22), hardness of heart and lethargy of soul are symptoms of disobedience in a Christian.

4. *Its cost is dear* (vv. 9–10). What a price one pays for the pleasures of sin for a season! It is strange how people can leave a partner they have loved and lived with for years, forgetting the shared struggles and joys and going unfaithfully with a smooth charmer. But it happens far too often. Trust and love, home and family, name and reputation, are lost in an episode of folly. Citizens in a democracy are taught today to insist on their "rights." However, as Christians we need to yield our rights to God and take our responsibilities more seriously. Insistence on rights alone tends to senseless revolution; fulfilling one's responsibilities brings revival.

5. *It leads to despair* (v. 11). Each of us has one short life. At most we have the privilege of a few decades of service to our eternal God. How sad if at the end we must regret a wasted life, devoured because we fell prey to our own lusts.

6. *Truth is distorted* (vv. 12–13). Quite often, we believe what we want to believe, using emotions not knowledge. We say, "There's none so blind as those who will not see." Often our opinions and beliefs change to suit our circumstances. Here, then, is the grave danger of immorality. Lowered stan-

dards become changed beliefs. We may talk about new insights of fresh understanding when in reality all we have are fickle excuses for our diluted Christian ideals. "Let God be true but every man a liar" (*see* Rom. 3:4). We must purposefully remain subject to the Word of God. No matter who tells us otherwise, God's standards are unchanging and must never be compromised.

7. *Believers are disunited* (v. 14). The wise writer of Proverbs (Solomon) here implied that he was openly on the brink of sin, while having fellowship with believers. How prayerfully we today must approach our life in the body of Christ, his church. If one brother or sister falls, the whole congregation is affected. A false move or the unguarded moment of one person may catastrophically change a church and limit its influence for years.

8. *God is disobeyed* (v. 21). No matter how compassionate we may feel toward the sinner, sin is still sin! Even if we call a particular sin "a sickness" or excuse it because of "extenuating circumstances," our holy God has eternally declared, "You shall not commit adultery." That is the final word on the matter. And when we disobey any of God's commands, we are in effect despising God and rejecting his authority in our lives.

9. *Lives are damaged* (v. 22). Immorality of either thought or deed produces a stain with an almost indelible quality. The blood of Christ may cleanse, but more than one life is affected adversely when someone is entrapped in sin. Failure is rarely final, but neither is it easy to forget. God may forgive the sinner, but those wronged will carry the scars of the injury. We remember David as a man "after God's own heart" who had great vision for God's purposes in most areas of his life. But we also see him as the repentant and anguished sinner who pitifully prayed Psalm 51.

10. *Man is destroyed* (v. 23). An outwardly successful man tearfully shared with a counselor that—for the short-lived flattering attentions of a younger woman—he had literally ruined his marriage, losing a faithful wife and all contact

with his three children. Can one doubt that his life was "destroyed" irrevocably?

Four Steps to Purity

Every married man—and every woman, too—ought to read Proverbs 5 very carefully at least once a month. We all need to be warned regularly about the perils of adultery and other sins of the flesh, including how best we can guard and protect ourselves. We are involved in a battle for purity that will be with us throughout our lives, but fortunately there are four strategies for achieving victory over lustful immorality.

Keep Clear

"Remove your way far from her, And do not go near the door of her house" (Prov. 5:8).

The Lord Jesus urged us to be ruthless against sin (Matt. 5:29–30). We must not trifle with it nor tolerate it in our midst. As the Israelites annually checked their possessions and cleared out any household leaven before the Passover, in like manner we should examine our homes and possessions. Do you have impure books, magazines, records, and papers that are available to hinder and pollute you if your care to go to them? If you must have television, determine to turn away your eyes "from looking at worthless things . . ." (Ps. 119:37). We are to think on whatsoever things are true, honest, just, pure, lovely, of good report, and have virtue and praise. The images of our mind are to be holy, not filled with evil imaginations. If we usually look on the opposite sex lustfully, it is time to spend much time in the Word and in pleading with God to make us pure. Only then we will "see God" (Matt. 5:8).

We must keep clear of temptations and avoid places where our eyes will wander, causing our minds to be stirred with base temptations. Let us cram our days with God-glorifying service instead. Try to avoid being alone with an unrelated member of the opposite sex in what may be compromising situations. Pastors and other counselors should be especially on guard when counseling anyone of the opposite sex if it is not possible to have a third party present. Let us be careful how we dress, behave, act, speak and look, wherever we are. We are not asked to be dowdy or cold-mannered, but to be modest. Ephesians 4:22–24 reminds us that in putting on "the new man" we become through Christ, we leave behind the lusts of our old selves.

Oh, to have the attitude of Joseph, who did not negotiate or stall when temptation came his way. He ran. He did not even go back to retrieve his cloak; he stayed far away from sin.

Keep Close

". . . rejoice with the wife of your youth. . . . And always be enraptured with her love" (Prov. 5:18–19).

God always gives a way of escape, so that we are able to bear the temptations that come our way. If you are married, you have the God-given privilege and duty to protect your spouse from the lure of the flatterer or flirt. A person's ministry will be marred or ruined if he or she is caught in this wicked trap. It is a blessed responsibility to protect our loved ones from such a pitfall, whether the sin be theirs or our own.

Pressures, circumstances, or the devil himself should not prevent you from meeting the needs of the one you have married. Pray together. Talk, listen, and love in word and deed. We all need unhurried time to chat and share the concerns of our lives. This means yielding our selfish motives—expect nothing, give all, and in honor prefer one another. It may someday be too late to say, "I'm sorry" and "I love you."

Keep All the Lord's Commandments

"For the ways of man are before the eyes of the LORD, and He ponders all his paths" (Prov. 5:21).

God gave us ten commandments. How dare we ignore a single one! It is impossible to hide from the presence of the

Lord. He sees into the secret recesses of our minds. But our desire to demonstrate our serious obedience of God's commands ought to be evident to everyone around us, too. Oh, that we would wage a war against lust! Our desire to demonstrate our serious obedience to God's commands ought to be evident to all.

Keep Clean

"He who covers his sin will not prosper, but whoever confesses and forsakes them will have mercy" (Prov. 28:13).

Praise God that he has provided a fountain to wash away uncleanliness. However much we have failed, the blood of Jesus Christ, God's Son, cleanses us from every sin. At any time or place, we come afresh to the Lord, claiming the washing from sin that his purifying blood provides:

> There is a fountain filled with blood
> Drawn from Immanuel's veins;
> And sinners, plunged beneath that flood,
> Lose all their guilty stains.

As sin and defeat are removed, we can start again. God can always change tragedy into triumph. Through David and Bathsheba, Solomon was born—he who later built the temple of God. The Lord Jesus did not come to condemn but to save. How beautifully he demonstrated this to the woman caught in adultery (*see* John 8:1–12). "Neither do I condemn you," he said. But he added the challenge to "go and sin no more."

16

Love, Lust, and License

> . . . he who commits sexual immorality sins against his own body. Or do you not know that your body is the temple of the Holy Spirit . . . ? (1 Cor. 6:18–19).

God created sex and pronounced it, along with all the rest of his creation, "good." Typical of man, however, is that he is guilty of wrecking and ruining every gift of God. Sexuality is no exception. This beautiful and precious gift, instead of being channeled as a lovely expression of mutual love between a husband and wife, has been the cause of broken dreams, marred lives, and even disease and death. Billy Graham has described ours as a "sex-crazed society." We have transformed something beautiful into an idol whose tarnished image becomes a master of deceit.

It is not that God has poured into us a strong sexual drive and then sadistically frustrated us by commanding "Thou shalt not. . . ." Not at all. Physical intimacy was intended to be the ultimate expression of love and companionship, the culminating act of two lives being brought together pleasurably in total union and commitment. It is so private and precious that it is to be reserved for the permanent, trusting, and sanctified relationship of marriage. God reserved sex for marriage to protect both male and female, as well as the children resulting from their union.

All people are aware that sexuality has been subject to widespread abuse. Our culture might outwardly excuse such malpractice, but it also knows that many reel under the devastating effects of openly flouting God's laws, all of which reflect what is best for society and for individuals. Countless lives are shattered daily as mankind chooses to indulge sexuality's call in ungodly ways. Rampant divorce, rape, sexual abuse of children, abortion mills, teenage pregnancies, escalating VD—including the death toll of AIDS—all these are *facts,* not just the emotional predictions of "moralizers." They are a sure sign that when a society wages war on nature, it can expect nature to counterattack.

A graphic biblical example of what is happening today is seen in the family of the great king of Israel, David. One of his sons, Amnon, lusted for his own half-sister, Tamar. What happened when he allowed his love to become lust and license is the preface to a tragedy involving rape and, eventually, murder and an attempted coup against the king. The story of Amnon's sin is found in 2 Samuel 13:1–19:

> Now after this it was so that Absalom the son of David had a lovely sister, whose name was Tamar; and Amnon the son of David loved her. Amnon was so distressed over his sister Tamar that he became sick; for she was a virgin. And it was improper for Amnon to do anything to her.
>
> But Amnon had a friend whose name was Jonadab, the son of Shimeah, David's brother. Now Jonadab was a very crafty man. And he said to him, "Why are you, the king's son, becoming thinner day after day? Will you not tell me?" And Amnon said to him, "I love Tamar, my brother Absalom's sister." So Jonadab said to him, "Lie down on your bed and pretend to be ill. And when your father comes to see you, say to him, 'Please let my sister Tamar come and give me food, and prepare the food in my sight, that I may see it and eat it from her hand.'"
>
> And David sent home to Tamar, saying, "Now go to your brother Amnon's house, and prepare food for him." So Tamar

went to her brother Amnon's house; and he was lying down. Then she took flour and kneaded it, made cakes in his sight, and baked the cakes. And she took the pan and placed them out before him, but he refused to eat. Then Amnon said, "Have everyone go out from me." And they all went out from him.

Then Amnon said to Tamar, "Bring the food into the bedroom, that I may eat from your hand." And Tamar took the cakes which she had made, and brought them to Amnon her brother in the bedroom. Now when she had brought them to him to eat, he took hold of her and said to her, "Come, lie with me, my sister." And she answered him, "No, my brother, do not force me, for no such thing should be done in Israel. Do not do this disgraceful thing! And I, where could I take my shame? . . ." However, he would not heed her voice; and being stronger than she, he forced her and lay with her.

Then Amnon hated her exceedingly, so that the hatred with which he hated her was greater than the love with which he had loved her. And Amnon said to her, "Arise, be gone!" And she said to him, "No indeed! This evil of sending me away is worse than the other that you did to me." But he would not listen to her. Then he called his servant who attended him, and said, "Here! Put this woman out, away from me, and bolt the door behind her." . . . Then Tamar put ashes on her head, and tore her robe of many colors that was on her, and laid her hand on her head and went away crying bitterly.

Lust and Loathing

There were five basic stages in this story of unbridled sexual passion, each of which has a counterpart in many of the meaningless relationships formed in today's love-and-leave culture.

1. *He lusted after her.* The series of events began in the mind. Sin always does. The Bible urges us to guard our mind and heart, being aware that what we think reveals what we are and often dictates what we do. Pornography, whether in magazines, tabloid newspapers, films or the innuendos of comedians, so degrades one's attitudes to sex that eventual-

ly lust is mistakenly identified as love. Those who feed on pornography will forget how to love, for love "thinks no evil" (1 Cor. 13:5).

Amnon lusted after Tamar, who—as his half-sister—was an improper object of his carnal affections. This was not love. There was no sense of responsibility here. Lust seeks to get; love seeks to give. Lust cannot wait; love is patient and loses consciousness of time. Lust is an inconsistent and irresponsible abuse of sex; love is utterly selfless and wants to please the loved one. Amnon began to dream, to fantasize about Tamar. He wanted to be alone with her to stir up his passion further. Lust was growing. It has to become the overwhelming motivation of his life.

There are three types of love: (1) I love you *because* you're good-looking, your daddy's rich, etc.; (2) I love you *if* you do this or that; and (3) I love you. *Period.* No conditions attached. Only the last is true love. It neither demands nor sets expectations. It gives freely. Amnon had none of this. He saw Tamar as an object, so his mind dwelled on what he could get from her.

2. *He lied to her.* Amnon's cousin devised a plan with which Amnon gladly agreed. (How easily we listen to evil companions! And how easily we blame another person for our own wrongdoing. We've been doing that since Adam tried to excuse his own sin in the Garden of Eden by saying to God, "The woman whom You gave to be with me, she gave me of the fruit of the tree, and I ate" [Gen. 3:12].) Amnon pretended to be ill, and when King David visited, his son said he was craving for some of Tamar's baked food. She eventually came to his supposed bed of sickness, where he repeated the lie by asking her to bake some cakes for him. Sin is always infectious. It spreads and multiplies. Here, lustfulness led to lying.

Many a boy has said to his girl, "I love you," when he really meant "I want you." Others pervert the truth by saying, "If you loved me, you would let me. . . ." A lovely relationship between a boy and a girl soon goes sour when the physical aspect of the friendship begins to dominate. The girl, especially, begins to wonder whether her boyfriend really loves her, or whether he is just "out to get what he can." Conversation stops. Instead of healthy fun, they just want to get away from the crowd and indulge their physical urges.

Tamar made the cakes, watched by her half-brother who mentally schemed and plotted as his lust grew. Amnon then ordered everyone out, to have Tamar all to himself. However, he was not really alone with her. There is an all-seeing eye that watches behind every closed door and in every dark corner. God saw all that Amnon did, for God can never be shut out. What about Tamar? One would have expected her to be aware of all that was happening. Maybe she was merely naive and innocent. Or did she feel flattered by her half-brother's attentions? Perhaps she, like others then and now, had almost a "death wish" within—a knowledge that trouble is at hand but a willingness to risk the consequences for the thrill of the moment. Whatever flashed through Tamar's mind, a moment of hesitation led to a lifetime of regret for her and the rest of David's family.

3. *He lay with her.* This was a clear case of rape, even if Tamar was legally of age, which she may not have been. Tamar tried to reason with her attacker, but her appeals reached neither his mind nor his conscience. Amnon's act was not just folly, but sin. (At such a time, crying aloud to God may not only bring strength to the victim, but may put back a reminder of God in the mind of the attacker.)

Although this story is specifically about a rape and an incestuous relationship, the Bible makes it clear that *all* sex-outside-marriage is sinful. There are to be three stages in every God-ordained relationship between a man and a woman: courtship, engagement, marriage. *Courtship* is a time of becoming acquainted with the other person's values, interests, likes and dislikes. For Christians, a sense of *fellowship* develops, uniting the spiritual part of each individual, the side that appreciates, worships, and enjoys God's company. During the courtship period, two people begin to come together mentally under God's direction. The *engagement* stage, after the couple have promised to make a final commitment to each other, is a time of *friendship* in the true sense of the word. The couple become more and more united in spirit and soul—in personality and character. It is a time of expectation and preparation for a life-long commitment.

The *marriage* vows affirm and mark the total *fusion* of a man and a woman. Now they become one in spirit, soul, *and* body. The tendency today is to reverse that order. Couples today often become one in body, then soul, then spirit. But that arrangement rarely lasts. When there is a sexual relationship before marriage, trust and security are undermined, which may eventually destroy the union. Having sex without the deep commitment defined in the marital vows cheapens the act itself and alters one's attitude toward self and partner. Premarital or extramarital intimacy devalues our sexuality so that it becomes selfish lust rather than selfless love. This can ultimately damage our relationship with our spouse and even our children. Having sex before marriage is like opening a Christmas present before December 25. Some of the wonderment is gone and can never be replaced.

Love is willing to wait until the approved moment. Restraint and self-discipline before the wedding form the foundations for loyalty, stability, and permanent unity within the marriage. "Many waters cannot quench love, nor can the floods drown it . . ." (Song of Sol. 8:7). Christians are not killjoys. God's patterns for love, sex, and marriage are given to protect us from tearing ourselves apart and suffering the trauma brought by the breakup of homes and families. That affects us all, especially the innocent! An attorney told about his difficult task of asking a child, whose parents were divorcing each other, which parent he wanted to live with. The boy tearfully answered that he wanted them both.

Living up to God's moral standards for using our sexuality often entails swimming against the tide of popular opinion. In previous generations, several practical considerations, or fears, kept individuals from immorality: (1) the fear of detection by others (today a new permissiveness exists); (2) the fear of conception (today many birth-control methods exist—though, tragically, some people even consider abortion to be one of them!); (3) the fear of infection (today's antibiotics can handle many sexually transmitted diseases—though *not* AIDS). But what happened to "the fear of God," which also implies respect and trust in his judgment and commands? Only a genuine fear of the Lord will prevent people from openly disobeying his laws. When one personally trusts Jesus Christ and commits submissively to him, Jesus gives the desire and power to obey. In so doing, he gives the joy that results from doing what is right. Amnon, like so many, impetuously gratified his own desires, but wrecked his prospects for the future and brought much trouble to his family. There *are* pleasures in sin, but only for a very short season.

4. *He loathed her.* What a realistic assessment of short-term pleasure seeking is found in verse 15: "Then Amnon hated her exceedingly, so that the hatred . . . was greater than the love with which he had loved her." Just a few moments of sin separated his intense "love" for Tamar from his deep hatred toward her. Amnon got what he wanted from Tamar, but it neither satisfied nor fulfilled him. It merely expressed the selfishness of his own life and brought him more unhappiness. Emptiness and bitterness are the symptoms of guilt.

The powerful emotion of love is easily injured. It is to be treated with respect and care so that when tested, the resources are sufficient to withstand all attacks and disappointment. Christians believe that God has a perfect plan for each life committed to him. Instead of scurrying round trying to find a "dream lover," Christians believe they can wait until God, through a variety of means, will guide them to the right life-partner. Slowly such a relationship blossoms as the couple enjoy each other's company. As they share mutual faith, they will enjoy reading the Bible, praying, and being involved with Christian activities together. There will be discipline and respect for each other, a desire for the other person's happiness. If physical pleasure is not allowed to dominate, they will be saved the frustration that petting brings. (Neither will there be the mutual contempt and loathing that all too easily follows an illicit surrender to physical passion.) Don't be fooled! Petting is invariably subject to the law-of-diminishing-returns. It is a natural set of stimuli that is part of the prelude to intercourse. It is not something you can stop easily. It drives you on, like a chain reaction. And it is not proper for even engaged couples to go so far that they cannot control their bodies.

5. *He left her.* Despite all Tamar's pleading, Amnon eventually called back his servant, who was then ordered to send her away. She had been treated only as a play object, so now she was discarded. However, this "toy" had a heart and emotions. Though Amnon may have hardened his already callous heart, Tamar's was broken. Eventually the whole tragic incident led to the murder of Amnon by his brother Absalom (2 Sam. 13:23–33) and indirectly to an attempted coup against King David (2 Sam. 15). Amnon's lust brought death, heartache, and treason to his family.

Christ and Compassion

For Amnon, all this happened because he allowed his brotherly relationship with Tamar to be corrupted by carnal urgings. Moral failure in the realm of sexuality is all too common and always has been! Some merely drift into situations that deep down they know are wrong, but they lack the willpower to do what is right. Others openly flout God's standards. Today it is generally considered acceptable to discuss the mechanics of what couples do, but not to ask whether it is right or wrong. However, even if attitudes change, God's commands do not. The Bible makes it clear that we are to "flee also youthful lusts" (2 Tim. 2:22). We are to keep ourselves pure. God will judge "fornicators and adulterers" (Heb. 13:4). And the call for sexual morality is an unchanging decree that applies to our actions and our attitudes. As Christ said, "Whoever looks at a woman to lust for her has already committed adultery with her in his heart" (Matt. 5:28).

All of us are guilty of sin to some degree or other, although all sins are not necessarily in the realm of sex. Unrighteous attitudes such as hypocrisy, pride, jealousy—and actions such as pilfering, lying, swearing, and disobedience—are harder to recognize as sin than blatant immorality.

It is significant that Christ was compassionate to the woman caught in the act of adultery. He also had compassion toward the Samaritan woman who, having already had five husbands, was then living with another man. In contrast, he was very severe toward the hypocritical arrogance of the religious leaders. The apostle Paul wrote to a group of young Christians in the wicked Greek city of Corinth, "Do not be deceived. Neither fornicators, nor idolaters, nor adulterers, nor homosexuals, nor sodomites, nor thieves, nor covetous, nor drunkards, nor revilers, nor extortioners will inherit the kingdom of God" (1 Cor. 6:9b–10). *But then he added:* "And such were some of you. But you were washed, but you were sanctified, but you were justified in the name of the Lord Jesus and by the Spirit of our God" (v. 11).

Christians do not claim to be without sin. Rather, as they admit their failure, they trust Christ to forgive and renew them. God, as man's Creator, had the right to lay down absolute and eternal standards of right and wrong. God, as man's Savior, provided a means to bring his wayward, sinful creation back to himself. For centuries, mankind had looked and longed for an adequate means of pardon so as to find peace with God. When God stepped down into the world to become a man, it was with the express purpose of dealing with sin, to reconcile man to God.

For thirty-three years the God-man, Jesus Christ, lived and was tempted to do wrong, just as we are, yet he never sinned. Even his enemies testified to his innocence. Christ was utterly pure in thought, word, and deed. He was a man of integrity who practiced what he preached and preached what he practiced. He showed love to the unlovely, cared for the rejected, welcomed the outcasts and underdogs. Above all, he gave mercy and forgiveness to the repentant and changed the lives of all who trusted him. He was God's expression of unconditional love.

Christ still brings that forgiving love to us. From the cross he reached down to a lost and sinful humanity, paying for the sin of every individual and thus providing a path for us to be brought back to God. We know that because he himself never sinned, it was impossible for death to hold on to Jesus Christ. He was raised from the dead and brought the promise of a totally new kind of life, victorious over death and all the powers of evil. The risen Jesus offers pardon and a new desire and power to do that which is right. We are commanded to:

BELIEVE that Christ died to cleanse us from sin; therefore we put our trust in him

REPENT of all sin—to break with it, whether sinful habits or evil relationships and dealings

RECEIVE Christ into our lives to cleanse us, conquer the evil within us, and control our actions. God promises that "if we confess our sins he is faithful and just to forgive us our sins and to cleanse us from all unrighteousness."

Will you personally claim the promises of God today? Ask God to be your Savior and Lord, and to cleanse, conquer, and control you.

17

The Backslider

> The backslider in heart will be filled with his own ways, but a good man will be satisfied from above (Prov. 14:14).

Backsliding is the cancer of Christianity. Why is it that we evangelical believers seem to have so little influence on those around us? Why isn't the world sitting up and taking note? The answer, basically, is that we are backsliding people. Even though we attend church regularly, something has gone wrong in our own lives. God spoke through the prophet Jeremiah and told us how he felt about backsliders:

> The LORD said also to me in the days of Josiah the king: "Have you seen what backsliding Israel has done? She has gone up on every high mountain and under every green tree, and there played the harlot. . . . Go and proclaim these words toward the north and say:
>
>> 'Return, backsliding Israel,' says the LORD,
>> 'And I will not cause My anger to fall on you;
>> For I am merciful,' says the LORD,
>> 'And I will not remain angry forever.
>> Only acknowledge your iniquity,
>> That you have transgressed
>>   against the LORD your God,

And have scattered your charms
To alien deities under every green tree,
And you have not obeyed My voice,'
    says the LORD.

"Return, O backsliding Israel," says the LORD; "for I am married to you. I will take you, one from a city and two from a family, and I will bring you to Zion. And I will give you shepherds according to My heart, who will feed you with knowledge and understanding. . . . In those days the house of Judah shall walk with the house of Israel, and they shall come together out of the land of the north to the land that I have given as an inheritance to your fathers" (Jer. 3:6, 12–15, 18).

What is a backslider? It is not merely a person who is anything *less* than once he was. In the eyes of God, a backslider is somebody who is not something *more* than once he was! As Christians we are to grow. We should be moving ahead and making progress, yet so many seem to slip into a rut and remain there, never making any advances spiritually.

How much progress have you made in the past year? Are there areas of victory that a year ago were areas of defeat? Is there new holiness? Is there a new love for God?

In the Scriptures there are many examples of people guilty of backsliding. Gideon led his small army and defeated the Midianites, but we never read of him gaining another victory. In fact, he gathered the gold and earrings the people gave him and built an ephod that became a snare to Gideon and the people of Israel. There was a time when he was doing great things for God, but soon that was gone. Is your Christian experience only a thing of the past? Do you look back on years recalling, "What great things I did for the Lord then!" or "How I spoke up for him!"? What about now?

Consider Samson, the man who had so many advantages. Physically strong, he killed a thousand with the jawbone of an ass. Yet he spent the last days of his life pushing and grinding with a millstone. He was blinded because he fell prey to his lust.

David is a man described as being "after God's own heart." Yet we see him falling into the most treacherous of sins. He committed adultery, and then contrived the murder of the woman's husband. He, too, was a backslider, as was Peter, who had said to Jesus, "If I have to die with You, I will not deny You!" (Mark 14:31). But within hours he had denied Christ three times.

How does backsliding begin? Whenever somebody suddenly appears to slip into open sin, there has previously been secret dabbling and trifling with sin, usually for weeks, months, or even years. I heard of a great pastor who was mightily used of God, until suddenly it all came to the fore that he had been committing adultery with one of his church members. When it came to trying to find out what had gone wrong, it was discovered that such things had been happening for years. This man had been sowing the seed of corruption and was now reaping the consequences.

Is there secret sin in your life? Maybe you think that nobody knows, or that it is excusable as "normal behavior." Sin *is* "normal" for mankind, but it is always hated by God. He never tolerates sin, never takes it for granted. God always loathes sin because he is holy and demands that we be holy, too. The process of backsliding often begins when we start to play around or trifle with a "little" sin. We look at or listen to wrong things. We begin to compromise our principles, and our resolve starts to wither away.

Backsliding starts at the closet door. In other words, when we cease to close the door on the world and regularly go apart to pray, Satan creeps in. How often do you pray? Is there an inward desire within you that forces you to that quiet place where you can be alone with God and hear his whisper? The devil would have us live for substitutes. The world spends time seeking honor, physical beauty, and material riches, but Christ denied himself all three. He "made himself of no reputation" (Phil. 2:7). "There is no beauty [in Him] that we should desire Him" (Isa. 53:2). "He was rich, yet for your sakes He became poor . . ." (2 Cor. 8:9). Subtly and slyly, Satan tries to start us searching for worldly things. We want to be thought well of by others and to climb the ladder of success. We all want "beauty," but too often the emphasis is on outward appearance rather than inner grace. Accumulation and riches are the pursuit of so many. How rarely in pulpits does anyone speak against money. The Lord Jesus spoke often about the futility of earthly treasures. He said, ". . . You cannot serve God and mammon" (Matt. 6:24) and that we are to sell what we have and give to the poor. We cannot ignore these teachings. So often we live off the fat of the land, but never seem to think of the millions starving because they lack both bread and the spiritual food of the gospel.

Symptoms of Backsliding

1. *A backslider has no spiritual appetite.* Like infants, backsliders are satisfied with milk, not solid food (1 Cor. 3:1–2). Do you have a desire for spiritual nourishment? Very rarely do people talk about their Bible study. Is your attitude, "God speak to me, teach and instruct me, show me something from your Word to make me more like Christ"? Or are you content to have just a nodding acquaintance with God? Are you satisfied with milk, or do you want to get to grips with the meat of what God says? We are suffering today because so many Christians are blown by every wind of doctrine. This is because we are not men and women who truly know the Word of God. We do not dig deep and grapple with the Scriptures. Therefore, when people come around and say something new, we follow them and go off on a tangent, and ultimately forget that Jesus Christ is the Way.

2. *The backslider has no desire for Christian fellowship.* In 2 Timothy 4:10, Paul wrote: "Demas has forsaken me, having loved this present world, and has departed for Thessalonica . . ." (a place known for its worldliness). Earlier we read of Demas's missionary journeys with Paul, but he left the apostle and went to a wicked city. When a person has lost that spiritual glow within and is not walking closely

with God day by day, he does not want to meet other Christians. Have you ever been like that? Perhaps you have met Christians who always have something fresh to say about the Lord's dealings with them—answers to prayer, people to whom they have witnessed, or something they have recently gleaned from the Word of God. Do you think, "I can't chat with them; they're too spiritual for me"? If sometimes you do not want to go to church, ask yourself, "Where is that desire that says, 'Would that there be more meetings, more Bible study, more prayer'?"

3. *The backslider has no spiritual growth.* In Hebrews 5:12, the writer says, "For though by this time you ought to be teachers, you need someone to teach you again the first principles of the oracles of God; and you have come to need milk and not solid food." Do you have somebody you are taking under your wing spiritually? Do you know a young believer whom you are seeking to nurture in the Christian faith? Are you desperate to grow closer to Jesus Christ? Alan Redpath once said, "The reason we do not fast is because we are not hungry for God." There should be that desire within you that says, "All right, never mind my normal routine. I'm going to go away and be apart with God; I am desperate for him." There ought to be a constant craving within us that says, "I want more of God." The believer's desire is to know God better each day. "As the deer pants for the water brooks, so pants my soul for You, O God" (Ps. 42:1). Nothing else, not his blessings, not the fruit that he brings, but he alone will satisfy.

4. *The backslider has no sense of dependence on God.* James spoke against those who say that tomorrow they will do this, and the next day they will do that (4:13). Instead, we ought to think, "If the Lord wills," we will act accordingly (v. 15). How many of your plans are man-made? Do you pray at the beginning of the day, "O God, take me where you want me to go today. Make my chance words be like arrows from you to the heart of the people to whom I speak"? On close inspection of the Book of Exodus, we see that Moses had to go up and down Mount Sinai like a yo-yo! On one occasion

God commanded, "Moses, come up." After the eighty-year-old man climbed up and got to the top, God said, "Moses, go down." What would your attitude have been? "Lord, you've just told me . . ."? Yet Moses did not complain; he simply obeyed. We need to learn to obey the Lord always, even if sometimes the command does not seem to fit in with our logic. Isaiah was told to go to tell King Hezekiah that he was going to die. Afterward, as the prophet was crossing the courtyard, going away from Hezekiah, God said, "Now, Isaiah, go back, and tell him he has fifteen more years to live." Isaiah did not know that Hezekiah had prayed, yet he returned to deliver the second message, in obedience to his God. He had a sense of ongoing dependence on God. Perhaps years ago you were called to the mission field. You knew you should have gone, but you did not. It is not too late to pray, "God, for years I've gone on my own path, but now I want to go where you send and do what you command."

5. *The backslider has no true happiness.* Psalm 51:12 says, "Restore to me the joy of Your salvation. . . ." If backsliders claim to be happy, I would argue that they are not really backsliders—they have *never* been the Lord's! A backslider is the most miserable of all people. Oswald Chambers prayed an unusual prayer saying, "Oh, God, take away from me all joy which does not come directly from the Lord Jesus." If you were to pray like that, how much joy would there be in your life? Is your joy based on what you can do for God? Is it dependent only on your family or your comforts, your health, your strengths? Or does it come from Christ?

6. *The backslider is a discouragement to others.* The backslider always seems to be criticizing others and grumbling. Remember that Christ said, "Hypocrite! First remove the plank from your own eye, and then you will see clearly to remove the speck out of your brother's eye" (Matt. 7:5). Are you known for your criticisms? Sometimes I tremble at the harshness and the hardness of some believers, who love to attack and destroy. That is the mark of a backslider. We need discernment, but not destroyers. Jesus said, "He who is

without sin among you, let him throw a stone at her [the adulteress] first" (John 8:7).

7. *The backslider does not examine himself.* Malachi said to the Israelites: "You have wearied the LORD with your words . . ." (2:17). It is so easy to point the finger at others and excuse ourselves. God never shows us more of other people's sin than he shows us of our own. If you see other people as worse than yourself, it is not of God. Rather, it is due to your own lack of self-examination. I once read a story of a poor homeless man who was asleep on a park bench when some mischievous youths came and rubbed moldy cheese in his beard. When he awoke, the man went around complaining that everybody smelled bad! When we are not walking with God, we excuse ourselves but find fault in everybody else.

8. *The backslider has no strength.* The prophet Jeremiah spoke God's warning that a lion would come down from the forests into the city and slay the people who had forsaken God (5:6). In other words, they did not have enough strength to defend themselves. What happens when you are tempted? Do you just give in, yield, and fall again? That is the mark of a backslider. Are you less than you once were? Are you failing to grow spiritually, so you are no stronger in God's grace than you once were?

The Results of Backsliding

Consequences for the Backslider

If a person has truly trusted Christ, he is secure forever. I may not believe in the perseverance of the saints, but I do believe in the perseverance of the Savior! He will never let go of anybody. Once we are his, we are his for all time. However, when a person backslides, he often falls into a sin that mars him and weakens his relationship with God. There is a limit on the amount of sin a Christian can commit—Galatians 5:17 says that the Spirit lusts against the flesh so it cannot do what it wants. Nevertheless, foolishness and failure become a backslider's bitter harvest.

Consequences for Others

The scars of sin not only mark a Christian's own life; they also pollute his witness to others. In Genesis we read of Lot in the city of Sodom. He was not dwelling where he ought to have been, and he was not mixing with God's people as he should. (There is a time when we should leave certain places and people.) Eventually Lot escaped, but in the process he lost his wife and his family. They had rebelled against God because Lot was a backslider. There is no guarantee that children of Christian parents will automatically grow up to know the Lord. Nevertheless, sometimes the cause can be traced to parental backsliding and compromise. One generation excuses sin in moderation; the next generation delights in it in excess. It is time we fell on our knees before God and cried that he would be merciful to us and would shower his understanding on those who looked for, but did not find, consistent godly witness in us.

Consequences Toward God

When David committed adultery with Bathsheba, a child was born who became sick. David earnestly prayed for God to save the child. God did not, because the sin had "given cause for my enemies to blaspheme" (2 Sam. 12:14). The world loves to see an inconsistent believer and to point a finger in ridicule. How many of us when witnessing have heard somebody say, "But such and such a Christian drinks, swears, and blasphemes God's name . . ."? As Paul told Timothy, "Take heed to yourself and to the doctrine. Continue in them, for in doing this you will save both yourself and those who hear you" (1 Tim. 4:16).

Restitution for the Backslider

Although a person may be a backslider and is not living for Christ as he ought God promises and provides a means of restitution, a way whereby the wayward one may come back to the fold.

First, there must be *acknowledgment* of backsliding: "He who covers his sins will not prosper, but whoever confesses and forsakes them will have mercy" (Prov. 28:13). In Jeremiah 2:19 we read: "'Your own wickedness will correct you, and your backslidings will reprove you. Know therefore and see that it is an evil and bitter thing that you have forsaken the LORD your God, and fear of Me is not in you,' says the Lord GOD of hosts." Notice that God did not forsake us, but we forsook him. Do you remember when, where, or how it happened? Come back to God, saying, "God, in such a place, at such a time, you know what I did, you know what went wrong. Now *I* acknowledge my backsliding."

Second, *turn* from backsliding. This may be harder than acknowledging it. It may mean paying back what was taken. It will involve sorting things out with a person you wronged. Perhaps something in your house will have to be gotten rid of. As a person acknowledges and turns from sin, God provides forgiveness. The way back for a backslider retraces the steps a person took to become a Christian. Again he must come to the cross. We trust Christ by saying to God, "I am a sinner and deserve hell. But take my sin, because your Son suffered and died and poured out his life to pay for my sin. Forgive me, and may the risen Jesus come and live within me." That, too, is what happens when a backslider is restored. He returns to the cross and says, "Your Son died not only for the sins of all the world, but for my personal sin of backsliding. Please forgive me. Come and live within me."

This renewal is seen in Peter's life after he slowly went away from his Master. He had such self-confidence that when he should have been praying with Jesus, he fell asleep and later fought with the energy of the flesh. He chopped off the ear of the high priest's servant in a misplaced attempt to defend Christ. A friend of mine says, "Peter was a preacher, but he chopped off an ear, instead of trying to win the ear with his words." It's an interesting thought, and many preachers today unfortunately use the same heavy-handed measures. We read that Peter followed Jesus afar off. Peter then mixed with the enemies of Christ until eventually he denied the Lord Jesus three times.

Do you deny Christ by your actions? Jesus was sympathetic and compassionate toward Peter. When the Lord Jesus was taken away, he "turned and looked at Peter" (Luke 22:61), knowing the apostle would deny him. What sort of look do you think it was? Not one of revenge or anger. It was a look of love, compassion, and concern. Later the angels who were at Jesus' tomb told the women to go and tell the disciples *and* Peter of the resurrection. Why did they specifically mention Peter? Was it not because he was the one who was so distraught over his denial of Christ? Eventually Peter met the risen Jesus. "Peter, do you love me?" was the thrice-repeated question Jesus asked him. Three times Peter denied Christ, but three times Christ gave Peter the opportunity to reaffirm his love, commitment, and dedication.

Are you a backslider? Come to the cross and say, "God, you know how I have sinned, and where I have sinned. As I lay my sin at the foot of the cross, deal with it, please. Wash me, fill me anew with your Holy Spirit, and help me to start to live again for you." He will restore to you "the years that the swarming locust has eaten" (Joel 2:25). Won't you come back to him now? Alexander Whyte rightly said, "The Christian life is a series of new beginnings." Begin again—now!

Protection from Backsliding

1. *Never neglect daily private prayer* (Heb. 11:6). We must meet with God and speak to him daily to undergird our faith. I find that if I neglect the secret place of prayer, it becomes hard to even keep a smile on my face. The Christian life must never allow drudgery to overshadow its delight.

2. *Never neglect daily, private Bible reading* (John 5:39). When we pray, we speak to God. When we read the Scripture, he speaks to us. Ask God to teach you something fresh from his Word each day. Like the Israelites gathering

the manna, collect it while it is still "resting on the dew," before it is contaminated by the world. Take the manna, feed on Christ by feeding on his Word.

3. *Do something for the Lord Jesus each day by serving others* (John 21:15). Seek daily to speak to an unsaved person about Christ. Give away a tract to the salesperson, the service-station attendant, your neighbors, and visitors. Put a gospel booklet in an envelope and send it to a friend. Do something for Christ by feeding his "lambs." Visit the sick, care for the lonely, be concerned about those whom nobody else is bothered about.

4. *Seek God's guidance in all you do* (Isa. 55:6). If you are in doubt as to whether something is right or wrong, seek God's blessing on it before proceeding. He is the Leader; we are his followers. Never go to a place where you would be embarrassed to be found by the Lord Jesus. Never say words that you would blush to speak if Christ was there listening. Remember, he *is* there!

5. *Follow no one but Christ* (John 8:12). The Lord is the One whose way you are to follow. Do what he would have you do; and live for him in all you do. Be consumed with a zeal for him. If fellow Christians have set a good and godly example, learn from them. I enjoy reading Christian biographies and have profited much thereby. As you see people's strengths, they make you desire to live as they did. But never just blindly follow Christians. They, too, may go astray. Your example is to be Christ.

6. *Never follow your feelings if they contradict the Word of God* (2 Cor. 4:2). It is often easy to be confused about our point of reference. I remember sitting at a railway station in a train waiting to leave. It was the 9:10 train on a Monday morning. I was there at 9:00 and was just musing and looking out the window when I saw that the train next to us had started to move. I looked again and thought, "No, it's not moving; *we* are." But then I was not sure. I was confused. What should I do? To find out, I quickly turned and looked at the platform. With that as a reference point, it was clear that we were standing still. Now it was obvious that it was

the other train moving. When it comes down to beliefs, our platform is the Word of God. That never moves! When people say there is a new emphasis, check it by the Word of God. Do not just rely on an isolated verse, but search out the weight of the Bible's teaching. Feed on the Word of God and Christ himself. Spend time with him daily and consider each new day as one when you could perhaps win somebody for him. There is joy in walking with Christ, but it is hard work trying to live as a Christian without spending time with him.

Have you stopped growing spiritually? Have you slipped? Are you a backslider? I beg you to come back to the cross. Claim the washing that Christ purchased with his own blood. Say, "Lord, from this day forth I am starting again." I urge you to also do something practical about that. Perhaps you need to write down the area of your life that needs to be altered. It may be helpful to share it with a dear Christian friend you can trust and ask him or her to check you in the future to see how you are getting on.

We are all sinners. The apostle Paul described himself as "the chief of sinners" and also "less than the least of all the saints." Let us first admit that we have not been what we ought to have been and then come back to Christ. Let us ask him to help us to start with a fresh beginning and, instead of being filled with our own ways, to be filled with "the fruits of righteousness" (Phil. 1:11).

18

Branded at the Door

And again another Scripture says, "They shall look on Him whom they pierced" (John 19:37).

God was never on the side of slavery, but, knowing the customs of the time, he gave careful instruction to Moses how a slave should be treated. Every Hebrew slave knew that after six years he could walk out from his master and be free. I imagine that the vast majority chose to do just that. Some, however, during their six years of servitude would grow to respect and love their master. For that minority, God gave an opportunity to so honor their master that they would yield their rights and remain slaves forever. All that they had or were or hoped to be was given over to their master:

> [The law given to Moses says:] "But if the servant plainly says, 'I love my master, my wife, and my children; I will not go out free,' then his master shall bring him to the judges. He shall also bring him to the door, or the doorpost, and his master shall pierce his ear with an awl; and he shall serve him forever" (Exod. 21:5–6).

To us, God's instructions on the matter seem very quaint. If a slave was to plainly declare that he loved his master and wanted to continue to serve him, he was to do something that was *personal* (nobody could force him), *public* (witnessed by the judges and always seen by everyone), *painful* (so it was off-putting to many people), and *permanent* (he could never retract his commitment).

The slave, in yielding all his rights to his master forever, was to stand against the doorpost of the master's house. There his ear was bored through with an awl to indicate his willingness to serve, although all he could expect to receive from his master was *provision* and *protection*. In essence, the slave was voluntarily branded to pledge his lifetime devotion. The few slaves who did this were going beyond their legal obligation of six years' service. By giving their very lives to their master, how they honored him! And all would notice their public testimony to the master's goodness.

Pierced for the Lord

Today we need to ask ourselves as believers whether we are likewise "branded at the door." Are we going beyond our legal obligations to the Lord? We can plainly declare that we love our Master by showing it in the realm of:

Devotions. Every Christian will develop that daily discipline of meeting with God. We will want to read the Bible and pray each day. (Will you go even further? Fasting is associated with earnestness in prayer.) Some of us are aware of great needs—spiritually poor towns and cities, unconverted children, needy missionaries, lack of real fruit in our own lives and in the lives of others. Let us be "branded" as Christ's servants and show our willingness to work in these areas by earnestly praying beyond our "legal obligation."

D. M. McIntyre followed three rules of prayer in his life: (1) pray till you truly pray; (2) pray till you are conscious of being heard; (3) pray till you receive an answer. This is a good pattern to follow.

Giving. Every believer has an obligation and privilege to

give to the Lord's work. Do we go *beyond* the church's stipulated tithe or "Lord's portion"? Do we follow the example of the widow, whose gift of two small coins was her entire fortune? It is so easy to believe that the Lord's people deserve the best when we think about our own affluence. There are, however, too many missionary societies that struggle financially and individual Christian workers who wonder where their next meal is coming from. Let us plainly declare that we love our Master by our sacrificial giving and lifestyle.

Use of Time. It is an amazing truth that our time can count for eternity. And it is frightening that time can be frittered away, never to be regained. Surely our Christian obligation is to support our churches, Sunday by Sunday, to pray in their prayer meetings and work enthusiastically for their regular projects. How easy it is for us to count the rest of our time as ours alone. Instead, let us pray for enabling to cram our days with that which will last for eternity. There are lonely people to be visited, letters to be written, souls to be won—time to be redeemed beyond our call to duty. May we always testify to our willingness to serve the Lord by how we set priorities in using our time.

Service. Although I knew her thirty years ago, I will never forget an elderly lady who was full of zealous good works toward everyone. What an impact her Christian service made on all those around her! May we twentieth-century believers be constantly seeking to meet the varied needs of others. Dawson Trotman, the founder of the Navigators, died in 1956 while trying to save two girls from drowning. He managed to push them into a rescue boat, even as he gasped his last breath. His obituary in *Time* magazine carried his photograph, under which were the telling words: "Always holding somebody up." The caring Christian will visit the sick and lonely, have a kind word for even the unlovely, and reach out a helping hand wherever a need is seen. It can be hard to leave the comforts of home and family to help others, but this plainly declares that we wear the brand of the Master and love him.

Soul-winning. Most of us feel that our duty is to talk to

those who *ask* about spiritual things. Should we not go even further to reach a perishing world? D. L. Moody never let a day go by without speaking to someone of his or her need of Christ. Let us pray that everyone we meet will be brought a step nearer to the Lord. Some will be miles away, others just a step away. Sometimes as we witness, we meet people who evidently have a prepared heart. Others will be hard to reach. But all need Christ. Being "branded at the door" in the realm of soul-winning means that like Wesley's evangelists we will be "out of breath pursuing souls." Every church should be full of soul-winners, willing servants of the Master!

Life's Work. Someone has said, "Only one thing matters in this passing world of sin; that our lives should tell for Jesus, be of some account for him." It is a sad reflection on Christianity that the number of missionaries is in decline. Are we branded as Christ's in the realm of our life's work? Well over a thousand Third World tribes are still unreached; countless villages, towns, and cities in Western Europe and the Americas are needing further evangelistic work. "Where are the reapers? Oh, who will come?" says the old hymn, but the need today is even greater than when those words were written.

A certain Mr. Crossley of Leeds was sixty-two years old when his wife, whom he had nursed for twelve years, died. His two children were either on or preparing for the mission field. Mr. Crossley saw an ad for an odd-job man to work with Sudan Interior Mission and decided to leave the prospect of retirement to take to the field for the Lord. It was then that he discovered he was suffering from liver cancer. He went to be with his Lord just days before he would have gone to the heart of Africa. How glad he must have been that he was willing to dedicate the final portion of his life's work to his Master.

Pierced for Our Sake

Our Lord never asks us to do what he himself would not have done. Exodus 21:5–6 is not only a picture of the believer, but also of Christ. He loved *his* "Master," God the Father, but he also loved his bride and children. When Christ died, he purchased for us a relationship with himself. Knowing Christ can be so intimate that it is like a marriage, with him as the bridegroom and his church as the bride. Or again, we become his sons and daughters.

Such is this all-encompassing love that he left heaven to come to earth as the Suffering Servant to die for us. Willingly he came to earth—going beyond his "legal duty." While we were yet sinners, Christ died for us. His was a personal, public, permanent, and painful work that branded him forever. Pierced by the nails at the cross after an earthly life of servitude, our Master died for sinners. As our exalted King, he richly provides for and protects those who are willing to go beyond their "legal duty" in giving over to him all that they have and are and hope to be.

> All my days and all my hours,
> All my will and all my powers,
> All the passion of my soul,
> Not a fragment but the whole,
> Shall be thine, dear Lord,
> Shall be THINE, dear Lord.

19

Conversion

[Jesus said:] "Most assuredly, I say to you, unless one is born again, he cannot see the kingdom of God" (John 3:3).

If you were a Christian living in Palestine at the time of Saul of Tarsus, you would do well to flee and hide. This deeply devout Jew was filled with bitterness and hatred over the new religion of those of his people who were following the risen Christ. Saul had obtained permission from the Jewish authorities to round up and imprison all believers as far away as Damascus in Syria, an important city about 150 miles away that had a large Jewish population. He had already participated in the stoning death of the first Christian martyr, Stephen (Acts 7:58; 8:1), and now had the taste for more Christian blood. Yet, after that fateful day on the Damascus Road, Saul's life would never be the same:

. . . suddenly a light shone around him from heaven. Then he fell to the ground, and heard a voice saying to him, "Saul, Saul, why are you persecuting Me?" And he said, "Who are You, Lord?" And the Lord said, "I am Jesus, whom you are persecuting. . . ." So he, trembling and astonished, said, "Lord, what do You want me to do?" And the Lord said to him, "Arise and go into the city, and you will be told what you must do." And the men who journeyed with him stood speechless, hearing a voice but seeing no one. Then Saul arose from the ground, and when his eyes were opened he saw no one. But they led him by the hand and brought him into Damascus. And he was three days without sight, and neither ate nor drank.

Now there was a certain disciple at Damascus named Ananias; and to him the Lord said in a vision. . . . "Arise and . . . inquire at the house of Judas for one called Saul of Tarsus, for behold, he is praying. And in a vision he has seen a man named Ananias coming in and putting his hand on him, so that he might receive his sight." Then Ananias answered, "Lord, I have heard from many about this man, how much harm he has done to Your saints in Jerusalem. . . ." But the Lord said to him, "Go, for his is a chosen vessel of Mine to bear My name before Gentiles, kings, and the children of Israel. For I will show him how many things he must suffer for My name's sake."

And Ananias went his way and entered the house; and laying his hands on him he said, "Brother Saul, the Lord Jesus, who appeared to you on the road as you came, has sent me that you may receive your sight and be filled with the Holy Spirit." Immediately there fell from his eyes something like scales, and he received his sight at once; and he arose and was baptized. And when he had received food, he was strengthened. Then Saul spent some days with the disciples at Damascus. Immediately he preached the Christ in the synagogues, that He is the Son of God. Then all who heard were amazed. . . . But Saul increased all the more in strength, and confounded the Jews who dwelt in Damascus, proving that this Jesus is the Christ (Acts 9:3–13, 15–22).

Visualize Saul's emotions as he traveled the road from Jerusalem to Damascus on what *he* considered a holy crusade. Surely there would be an intense look in his eyes! If he was riding a horse, his spurs were no doubt digging deeply into the flesh of the wearied animal. Saul was determined to reach Damascus as rapidly as possible, and his entourage was probably under orders from this angry man that there was to be no let-up. But when that voice came from above,

Saul fell to the ground in surrender, unaware as yet that a new man was being born within him, although his response—"Who are You, Lord?"—indicates that he knew he was being addressed by the deity.

Saul had a meeting with God that he never forgot. There was a complete turnaround in his nature—even his name changed. Saul, who became Paul, perhaps the most influential Christian missionary of all times, was born again! His self-centered concerns were tossed away and replaced by godly altruism.

Conversion Changes

Both the apostle's writings and the biblical passages that describe his experiences testify to five basic changes that Christ brought into Saul/Paul's life. They are characteristics of all true Christian conversions.

1. *He prayed.* God used Saul's prayerfulness to convince Ananias and other Christians that Saul had been truly converted. The Lord said, "Behold, he is praying." Before conversion, people use prayer as an emergency ripcord in times of emergency. "Lord, help me get through this exam" or "Lord, please heal my wife" come readily to the lips of even those who would not normally pray. However, once a person is adopted into God's family—the body of believers—it becomes the most natural thing in the world to desire to talk with God the heavenly Father. Prayer is the Christian's vital breath. It becomes the spontaneous expression of gratitude and servitude to God.

Do you pray regularly with thanksgiving and praise? If not, I humbly suggest that you have never been converted. As Christian maturity develops, all believers find that from their waking thoughts to the closing moments of each day, there is an inward desire to communicate with the living God in prayer.

2. *He practiced the Lord's will.* Where a loving relationship exists, a desire to please one's partner becomes an overriding concern. Within days of his Damascus Road experi-

ence, Saul was baptized. This was an outward expression of the inward miracle that had taken place. Baptism does not make a person a Christian, but it is a badge of discipleship that signifies a covenant with God. Jesus commanded it (Mark 16:16), so the new convert complied. Obedience delayed is disobedience.

While still a student, F. B. Meyer woke early one morning and looked out of the window in his residence hall. He noticed a light in the room of young C. T. Studd, the England cricketer who eventually became a missionary. "What were you doing up so early?" asked Meyer later that day.

"Last night I read the words of Jesus, 'If you love me, keep my commandments.' Since I *do* love Jesus, I got up to go through the Gospels to make sure I was keeping them," explained Studd.

That is one's attitude after conversion. Are you up-to-date on your obedience to Christ? When did something change in your behavior simply because Christ commanded you to act differently? If there is no such desire to live to become more like Christ, perhaps it is because you have never really been "born again."

3. *He preached.* We read in Acts 9 that the newly converted Saul/Paul immediately "preached the Christ in the synagogues, that He is the Son of God" (v. 20). Anywhere and at all times, the Christian will want to chatter about his or her beloved Savior. Similarly, you can always recognize a newly engaged woman by the way she seeks to display the ring on the third finger of her left hand as she tells you all about her husband-to-be. Or ask her male counterpart about his fiancée and he will talk *ad infinitum* about her, extolling her virtues and boasting of the depths of their mutual love. Greater love has no one seen than that displayed when Christ died to save us, we who were rebels against all he represented. How, then, can a true believer keep silent about the Master? Among true converts there will be a desire to speak to others about eternity and the need to settle things with their Creator God. The task of proclaiming Christ is not just the job of professional preach-

ers, but is a responsibility of every converted man, woman, and child.

4. *He was persecuted.* After his conversion, Saul the Hunter became Paul the Hunted. It was not long before "the Jews plotted to kill him" (Acts 9:23). Paul's was to be a life of suffering and persecution, yet he found a contentment and joy in serving Christ that outweighed everything else.

Jesus never promised an easy road, but rather the opposite. He said, "If anyone desires to come after Me, let him deny himself, and take up his cross, and follow Me" (Matt. 16:24). If people hate and fear Christ, the King of Glory, it is inevitable that they will persecute his followers. In certain places, particularly in Islamic and Communist countries, Christians are still persecuted. Even in Western countries, times can be hard for those who faithfully stand alone against the tides of humanism, compromise, and worldliness. Just because the public overwhelmingly speaks favorably of an individual does not mean that God is pleased with that person. Most likely, the opposite is true! People who try to live in conformity with God's commands will find pressure is put on them to lower their standards: ". . . all who desire to live godly in Christ Jesus will suffer persecution" (2 Tim. 3:12).

5. *He knew the presence of God within him.* As soon as a person receives Christ as Savior and Lord, God's Holy Spirit comes to live within that new life. A Christian's body becomes the dwellingplace of God. In fact, God has promised that his presence will go before, behind, beside, below, above, and will abide within all who trust him. Paul felt this presence (Acts 9:17b), as may all who are made right with God through the work of Jesus Christ.

Are You Converted?

Are these five characteristics true of you? Are you really converted—"born again . . . through the word of God which lives and abides forever" (1 Peter 1:23)? The worst offenders may be converted. Christ did not come into the world to call the righteous, but to save sinners. For three years through-out the earthly ministry of Jesus, an air of generosity and kindness was felt in the land. Whole families, neighbor-hoods, and towns were blessed when previously blind, deranged, leprous, or sinful people returned home, com-pletely restored by their contact with Jesus Christ. Saul the Persecutor would have met people who had been changed by the power of Christ and would have known of Christ's great influence in the lives of many. But just as the same sun that melts butter can harden cement, the same Gospel that was blessing thousands appeared to harden the heart of Saul against the Lord. When he had the opportunity to help at the stoning of Stephen, Saul gladly participated by guarding the coats of those who threw the stones. Eventually Stephen's prayer, "Father, forgive them," was to be answered in the life of Saul.

In no way would we describe Saul as "good," yet he was converted. Later he was to remind the morally lax group of believers in Corinth: ". . . But you were washed, but you were sanctified, but you were justified in the name of the Lord Jesus and by the Spirit of our God" (1 Cor. 6:11).

Whoever you are, whatever you have done, however you have lived, you can be converted to Jesus Christ, the way, the truth, and the life. None are too far from God to be for-given and inwardly changed. John Wesley, the great evange-list and founder of Methodism, knew this when he wrote in his journal: "We came to Newcastle about six, and walked into the town. I was surprised: so much drunkenness, curs-ing and swearing (even from the mouths of little children) do I never remember to have seen and heard before, in so small a compass of time. Surely this place is ripe for Him who 'came not to call the righteous, but sinners to repentance.'"

The first step in trusting Christ is to recognize our need because of the wrong that lies within. The worst sinner needs to be converted but even the most "devout" need con-version. When the religious leader Nicodemus approached Christ at night, so as not to be seen by his associates, Jesus said, "You must be born again." A display of piety is not sufficient to deal with sin and bring a person to God. It can lead to fanaticism rather than real faith.

Basically, all religions have to do with people's attempts to reach up to God and understand his purposes. God, though, is too big and holy for small, sinful man to attain on his own. Instead, God has stooped down to this earth to reach, rescue, and redeem mankind. If you question some so-called Christians about their spiritual life, you will find they are not certain of sins forgiven, peace with God, or the certainty of heaven, *unless* they are trusting in Christ alone to save them. True Christian experience is founded on faith in Christ's redemptive powers, not in "trying to be good." It involves a relationship with God, not a complicated ritual and set of rules.

Saul was a deeply religious Jew. He called himself "a Hebrew of the Hebrews; concerning the law, a Pharisee" (Phil. 3:5), which for him meant that he kept the 613 commandments that the religious experts had devised. He would tithe, fast, pray, and eat separately from non-Pharisees and would be well respected as a religious authority. But he needed to be converted to the true religion born of Christ's death and resurrection.

John Berridge was an eighteenth-century Anglican clergyman and a great evangelist. Though he died two centuries ago, in his epitaph he still testifies of the power of the gospel:

> Here lay the earthly Remains of JOHN BERRIDGE
> late Vicar of Everton and an itinerant Servant
> of JESUS CHRIST who loved his Master and his Work
> and after running on his Errands many Years was
> called up to wait on Him above. Reader art thou born
> again?
> No salvation without new birth.
> I was born in sin Feb 1716
> Remained ignorant of my fallen State till 1730
> Lived proudly on Faith and Works for Salvation
> till 1754
> Admitted to Everton Vicarage 1755

Fled to JESUS alone for refuge 1756
Fell asleep in Christ Jan 1793.

Piety and "good works" do not work salvation. The Bible says, "For by grace you have been saved through faith, and that not of yourselves; it is the gift of God, not of works, lest anyone should boast" (Eph. 2:8–9). And again: "Not by works of righteousness which we have done, but according to His mercy He saved us, through the washing of regeneration and renewing of the Holy Spirit" (Titus 3:5). Jesus said, "Assuredly, I say to you, unless you are converted and become as little children, you will by no means enter the kingdom of heaven" (Matt. 18:3). Have *you* been converted?

Three Vital Steps

You Must Turn from Sin

Conversion starts with an act of the will. Biblically, it is called "repentance." This is *not* an emotion, a general feeling of regretting past sins, but a deliberate act of turning one's back on all that is wrong. It means renouncing sinful practices and habits—past, present, and future. The Bible teaches that there is one sorrow for sin that does not bring blessing, but another that leads to eternal life. Judas, who betrayed Christ, was full of regret and remorse, but he did not repent. But Peter, who denied Christ, had *godly* sorrow and was forgiven.

Seven characteristics of true repentance are listed in 2 Corinthians 7:10–11:

> For godly sorrow produces repentance to salvation, not to be regretted; but the sorrow of the world produces death. For observe this very thing, that you sorrowed in a godly manner:
>
> > What diligence it produced in you,
> > what clearing of yourselves,

what indignation,
what fear,
what vehement desire,
what zeal,
what vindication!

In all things you proved yourselves to be clear in this matter.

All seven qualities speak of an anger at oneself for having sinned and a real desire to turn from wrongdoing. Are you truly sorry for the sin in your life? Have you ever repented by telling God of your wrong and asking him to change you? John the Baptist, the Lord Jesus, Peter and Paul, all began their ministry by preaching repentance. It is all-important for salvation.

You Must Turn to Christ

This is an act of the mind and the heart. After repentance, there is faith in God's power, wisdom, and love. I remember leading a beach mission with children on the sands of Scarborough, North Yorkshire. We had had a tug of war, some choruses, and then were enjoying a quiz, when suddenly a Royal Air Force Lightning jet flew by, skimming the surface of the sea before it turned and flew inland. A minute or two later it returned and went into steep incline over Scarborough Castle. I thought the pilot was doing a stunt.

Then, to our horror, the plane flipped and dramatically dropped into the sea. It crashed less than 200 yards away from the beach. The plane disintegrated on impact. The pilot was killed instantly. The headline in the newspaper the next day way, "Pilot gives life to save crowds." It described how, instead of ejecting from the plane and risking its crashing onto the crowded holiday beach, the pilot had made an instant decision to stay with the stricken plane and steer it away from the crowds. He sacrificed his life to save us, although the pilot had probably not anticipated certain death in such tragic circumstances. In contrast, however, the Lord Jesus deliberately left heaven and came to earth with the express intention of going to a death where he would "save the crowds."

Think of all the history of sin in this world. All human lives have been marred by sin. Christ took all that sin on the cross. He bore public sins and private sins. Christ paid for the sins that have made us as well as those we love miserable. He has the power to forgive our sins. The Bible speaks of sins being cast behind God's back, or being removed as far from us as the east is from the west, or being cast into the depths of the ocean, or being blotted out completely! Christ loved us and gave himself for us. Now he is risen and we need to turn to him in repentance and faith.

God Turns to You

This is an act of God. It signifies Christian conversion, or regeneration. As soon as someone is genuinely repentant and believes in Christ's sacrificial death, God works a miracle within that person to forgive sin and take control. God takes up residence and becomes Master and Guide of his or her life. Immediately sins are forgiven and there comes a peace and joy that the world's pleasures can never imitate. The new Christian is made right with God for eternity.

I remember reading the report of the American helicopter pilot who was sent to rescue the stricken crew in the *Union Star* ship off the coast of Cornwall. He described the highest waves and worst conditions he had ever flown in. He hovered above the boat and let down a rope to the men whose faces he could see as they stayed in the cabin on deck. None of them moved toward the rope. Eventually, trying to urge them to take the rope and be lifted to safety, the pilot dragged the rope across the deck. Nobody took it. "They had no sense of urgency," he said. The heartsick pilot had to leave. All the crew members were lost.

Have you been converted? There is no time to lose! "Behold, now is the accepted time; behold, now is the day of salvation" (2 Cor. 6:2b). If you have never been converted, now is the moment to repent and believe. Ask Christ to forgive and change you. He will turn to you. He has promised to do so. "Therefore, if anyone is in Christ, he is a new creation; old things have passed away; behold, all things have become new" (2 Cor. 5:17).

20

The Blood of the Lamb

> "I will ransom them from the power of the grave; I will redeem them from death . . ." (Hos. 13:14).

I know this is a personal question, but do you sleep well at night? Let me ask further: if you were the eldest boy in your family, would you be able to sleep peaceably knowing that an angel of death was due to kill all the firstborn sons in the land? Would your parents sleep well that night? It is possible to sleep well, even on such a night—because God made a way whereby you can be absolutely safe, despite the awful things that might happen.

Centuries ago, the angel of death visited the neighborhood of the enslaved Israelites in Egypt. But the divine protection of their holy God lay over them, and they were saved because they obeyed the Lord's commands:

> Now the LORD spoke to Moses and Aaron in the land of Egypt, saying, ". . . Speak to all the congregation of Israel, saying: 'On the tenth day of this month every man shall take for himself a lamb. . . . Your lamb shall be without blemish, a male of the first year. You may take it from the sheep or from the goats. Now you shall keep it until the fourteenth day of the same month. Then the whole assembly of the congrega-

tion of Israel shall kill it at twilight. And they shall take some of the blood and put it on the two doorposts and on the lintel of the houses where they eat it. Then they shall eat the flesh on that night; roasted in fire, with unleavened bread and with bitter herbs they shall eat it. . . . And thus you shall eat it: with a belt on your waist, your sandals on your feet, and your staff in your hand. So you shall eat it in haste. It is the LORD'S Passover. For I will pass through the land of Egypt on that night, and will strike all the firstborn in the land of Egypt, both man and beast; and against all the gods of Egypt I will execute judgment: I am the LORD. Now the blood shall be a sign for you on the houses where you are. And when I see the blood, I will pass over you; and the plague shall not be on you to destroy you when I strike the land of Egypt. So this day shall be to you a memorial; and you shall keep it as a feast to the LORD throughout your generations. . . . So you shall observe the Feast of Unleavened Bread, for on this same day I will have brought your armies out of the land of Egypt. Therefore you shall observe this day throughout your generations as an everlasting ordinance. . . .'"

Then Moses called for all the elders of Israel and [told them all the Lord had said]. So the people bowed their heads and worshipped. Then the children of Israel went away and did so; just as the LORD had commanded Moses and Aaron, so they did.

And it came to pass at midnight that the LORD struck all the firstborn in the land of Egypt, from the firstborn of Pharaoh who sat on his throne to the firstborn of the captive who was in the dungeon, and all the firstborn of the livestock. So Pharaoh rose in the night, he, all his servants, and all the Egyptians; and there was a great cry in Egypt, for there was not a house where there was not one dead. Then he called for Moses and Aaron by night, and said, "Rise and go out from among my people, both you and the children of Israel. And go, serve the Lord as you have said" (Exod. 12:1, 3, 5–8, 11–14, 17, 21, 27b–31).

For over four hundred years, since the days of Joseph, the nation of Israel had been slaves in Egypt. God's plan was for Moses to lead the people out to the Promised Land. As slaves, they dreaded being treated badly by the Pharaoh, but when Moses made the request for their freedom to leave, things became even worse. God sent a series of plagues that demonstrated that it was his intention that the Israelites be released. Each time, the Pharaoh pleaded for mercy, but the Israelites were not allowed to leave—until God sent one final devastating plague.

Warning was given to the Israelites that at midnight on the fourteenth day of the first month, an angel of destruction would pass throughout the land and all the firstborn sons would die. But, along with the warning, God also gave a way of protection. The Israelites were told to take a lamb on the tenth day, keep it as part of the household until the fourteenth day, and then kill it to eat. Some of the blood from the lamb was to be sprinkled on the lintel and doorposts of their houses. God said, "When I see the blood, I will pass over you."

Deliverance for Israel

Every Israelite family could go to sleep that night, absolutely certain that their firstborn would awaken in the morning. The angel of death need not worry them because of three factors:

1. *The blood of the lamb.* If the Egyptians had looked on, they might well have thought the talisman of daubed blood to be ridiculous, but God had a plan, as always. Sin brings death, so in every household in Egypt there was death—of either a sinner or a substitute: either the firstborn son or a lamb. The fact of the blood kept the Israelites safe; they could rely on it for security and protection.

2. *The promise of God.* The Lord God had said, "When I see the blood, I will pass over you." He did not say, "I may pass over you," but "I will." This was a clear-cut, straightforward promise. God's very nature makes it impossible to lie, so we can trust his promises.

3. *The act of faith.* There was a step of obedience that all who would be protected had to take. Faith was to be demonstrated by sprinkling blood on the doorposts. That simple

step made all the difference between life and death for the Israelites in bondage.

The day after that unforgettable midnight, there was great weeping throughout Egyptian households. From the Pharaoh in his palace to the prisoner in his dungeon, first-born sons had died. Only the Israelites were safe—because by faith they had relied on the blood of the lamb and the promises of God.

Deliverance for the Christian

"Men fear death as children fear to go in the dark," said Francis Bacon. Is that how you feel? Is it possible to face the inevitable ending to our days on earth with acceptance, even confidence? Yes! A wise old woman of the Old Testament said, "We will surely die and become like water spilled on the ground, which cannot be gathered up again. Yet God does not take away a life; but He devises means, so that His banished ones are not expelled from Him" (2 Sam. 14:14). To face death with serenity, you must trust in the Lord's provision by relying on the same three things that sustained the Israelites so long ago in Egypt:

1. *The blood of the Lamb.* All the lambs sacrificed to the Lord God in Old Testament days were a prophetic picture of the fact that one day God's Son would come to earth to die like an innocent lamb as a sacrifice for sin. John the Baptist called Jesus "the Lamb of God who takes away the sin of the world." This could be applied to Jesus not only because he was young, male, and without blemish, as sacrificial lambs had to be, but because he was to die as our substitute, in payment for our sins. He carried our guilt and our shame so that we might be forgiven and spared eternal death.

The Bible tells us much about the blood of Jesus Christ. It is God's "own blood" (Acts 20:28). Christians are "justified by His blood" (Rom. 5:9). We "have redemption through His blood" (Eph. 1:7), that is, Christ shed his blood to bring us back to God, to reconcile us to our Creator. The blood of Jesus Christ "cleanses us" (1 John 1:7) and has "washed us from our sins" (Rev. 1:5). It sanctifies us (Heb. 13:12), giving us the boldness to approach the throne of God (Heb. 10:19) and victory over Satan, the great deceiver (Rev. 12:9–11).

The implications and blessings that flowed from Christ's death on the cross were enormous. There he took onto himself the venom and poison that create the fear of death and hell. He has died so you and I can be forgiven. He has risen so we can enjoy his everlasting presence. If we are trusting in the finished work of Christ, we need fear no evil, not even the sting of death.

2. *The promises of God.* Repeatedly throughout God's Word, there are many exceedingly great and precious promises that assure all who believe in Christ that they are his forever. It would be a foolhardy rejection of God to doubt him after he has made his promises so clear. Here are a few:

"For 'whoever calls upon the name of the LORD shall be saved'" (Rom. 10:13; cf. Joel 2:32).

"If you confess with your mouth the Lord Jesus and believe in your heart that God has raised Him from the dead, you will be saved" (Rom. 10:9).

"He who has the Son has life; he who does not have the Son of God does not have life" (1 John 5:12).

"If we confess our sins, He is faithful and just to forgive us our sins and to cleanse us from all unrighteousness" (1 John 1:9).

If ever one fears, one need simply claim and rely on any and all of these promises. Imagine that you were promised a gift of a Rolls-Royce by a good friend. Just before the stated delivery date, suppose that you went out to buy an old, battered, used car because you doubted your friend would be true to his word. Your friend would have every reason to feel grieved. Yet the God who *always* keeps his promises has pledged eternal life on the basis of Christ's death. Why should we doubt and deeply grieve him?

3. *Our act of faith.* There must be a step of actual commitment to Christ. The Bible speaks of Christian conversion, of being born again or born from above as a new creation. Have you ever taken that step, whereby you have turned from

your sin to trust Christ as your Savior and Lord? Being born into a so-called Christian country, going to church, being baptized, or doing your best does not do the trick. In fact, there is no trick to it. There is, though, an abiding relationship with God to be gained. Are you absolutely sure that you have asked Jesus Christ to be your Savior and Lord? If not, why not? And if not, why not do something about it now?

There is a legend connected with the Exodus account that concerns a godly Jewish father and mother and their large family. It was the first Passover night. They had all gathered for the ceremonial meal as God had commanded. The bowl with the lamb's blood was in the center. The hyssop branch, to be used like a paintbrush, lay next to it. They all prayed and prepared for what God had promised would be their last sleep in their Egyptian home. The quietness of the night, however, was disturbed because the youngest daughter—a little girl—felt concerned about her oldest brother. *Would he be all right?* she wondered. Would the angel of death see the blood on the doorposts and pass over? Time and again she woke her father, seeking reassurance. Just before midnight, she again was fearful and went to shake her sleeping father, who was irritated at his daughter's lack of faith. "It is all right; God has promised," he said.

"Are you sure the blood is clear enough to see?" asked the little girl.

This time, the father got up from his mat, took the girl by the hand, and led her through the room to the door. He opened it, went out and pointed his hand to the lintel and doorposts. He was about to say, "Look," when he was shocked and silenced by the sight. There was no blood at all! Instantly and in panic, he dropped his daughter's hand and ran to the table where still lay the bowl, the blood, and the hyssop. In all the preparation for leaving the land and for the journey ahead, the most important thing had been neglected. Just in time, the blood was sprinkled around the doorway and the firstborn son was safe. The legend says that it was God who kept waking the girl to prompt the father to comply with God's instructions.

I would urge you to check that you are trusting in the fact that Christ's blood was shed for you and that you are relying on the promises of God for your eternal safety. Have you made that crucial act of faith whereby you have put your trust and confidence in the Lord Jesus?

Many centuries after that first Passover, an old man was imprisoned in a cell in the city of Rome. If we were to obtain permission to visit him, we would need a flaming torch to show us the way as we descend the steep steps to the dark, damp dungeon. An old door would creak open. Incarcerated in a corner of a cell would be the aged prisoner, fetters cutting into his wrists and ankles. His back had been lacerated by receiving the thirty-nine stripes five times. (I make that one hundred and ninety-five stripes in all!) Three times he had been beaten by rods. Three times he had experienced shipwreck, and once he had been in the deep for a day and a night. He had suffered hunger and nakedness. He had lived in peril of thieves, robbers, his own faithless countrymen, and ungodly people from other nations. Yet still there was peace and contentment written over his face. Holding the torch close to his face, we would see a not-so-attractive man, but as he pushed back his silver hair the radiance and joy of the man would be apparent. He was facing imminent execution at the hands of Nero, yet still there was joy. Ask him how he could have such joy, and he would reply, "The time of my departure is at hand" (2 Tim. 4:6b). He was soon to be visited by the angel of death, but he does not fear. In fact, he is eagerly anticipating it.

Over thirty years before, traveling on the road to Damascus and intending to round up and persecute believers, this man had met the living, risen Christ. Instead of relying on his religious works to save him, and recognizing his sinful bitterness toward those who differed with him, he came to the moment of conversion whereby he trusted in the blood of the Lamb, claimed the promises of God, and made his act of faith. Saul the Persecutor willingly became Paul the Persecuted, for the Lord's sake.

Paul did not fear death. Normally he used other words,

such as "departure" or "sleep" or "absent from the body." It is as if he took the idea of death and trampled it under foot in the muddy dungeon, knowing that Christ's death and resurrection had defeated death forever. The last enemy, death, need not be feared. Nail-pierced hands welcome all who will trust Christ. He will take all believers through the valley of the shadow of death to be with him forever.

21

Christ, the Answer

> And my God shall supply all your need according to His
> riches in glory by Christ Jesus (Phil. 4:19).

What does everyone have in common? The answer is simple. Rich or poor, black or white, young or old, everyone has
problems. Behind the smiles or the busyness of life, we all
face issues we wish we could solve or avoid. The newspaper
"advice columns" attest to the variety of questions we
humans face on a daily basis—ranging from "Does he really
love me?" or getting along with a meddling in-law or dealing
with a family member's alcohol addiction. Some problems
are relatively trivial in that they are temporary and "serious" only to the person facing them. But we all struggle with
bigger and more long-term questions to one degree or another. Three concerns are universal:

1. *The problem of suffering.* Very few of us are immune
from suffering of some type. Centuries ago, a wealthy,
respected man called Job lost his business, his health, and
most of his family in a matter of days. It was cold comfort to
hear: "Yet man is born to trouble, as the sparks fly upward"
(Job 5:7). Whether it is the millions starving in different
parts of the world, a child with a dreadful disease, a linger-

ing illness, a bitter conscience, a major regret, or a serious loss, suffering of one sort or another is everywhere. Sometimes we blame ourselves. Often we blame God and wonder why he allows bad things to happen to "good people."

Is there an answer to the problem of suffering?

2. *The problem of sin.* The words S-I-N and G-U-I-L-T both have "I" in the middle. Sin occurs when we ignore God's laws and live for number one rather than for God—and therefore for others. God our Maker has given us commands that we fail to keep. We think wrong thoughts, speak wrong words, and do wrong deeds. Although we may be respectable in the world's eyes, our hearts are really at enmity with God. If there were no sin in the world, there would be no wars or starvation, no need to lock our homes or cars, no fears in the streets, no pornography or smutty television, no arguments or lost tempers, no divorce or drunkenness. Violence, AIDS, abortion, and crime would be unknown.

Sin is definitely a problem for all of us. Is there an answer to it?

3. *The problem of death.* One hundred out of every hundred babies born will die eventually. It is the ultimate statistic. Life rapidly rolls by. Time is short. Our years have been likened to a vapor (Ps. 39:5), to grass or a flower (Ps. 103:15; Isa. 40:7)—all here today but gone tomorrow.

When the news goes round that you have "gone," what will be your destination? What happens when a person dies? The Bible teaches that "it is appointed for men to die once, but after this the judgment" (Heb. 9:27). Why do people go jogging, or take vitamin tablets, or have regular medical checkups? Behind it all is a fear of death. Everything we achieve on earth—fame, fun, friends, and fortune—has to be left behind. However much we leave in our will, we leave everything the world values. The only item we take with us is a record of the life we have lived and of what we have done with Jesus Christ.

How different life would be if only there was an answer to the problems of sin, suffering, and death! But there *is* an answer!

ıtion

ne man who never needed to face the problems of suffering, sin, or death has ever been born into this world. That man was Jesus Christ, who cares for us in all our problems and can help us cope with them. His love was so great that he left heaven and came to earth as a man. God had every right to wash his hands of the world that was in rebellion against him, but instead he came to deal with our sin, suffering, and death.

Christ Deals with Suffering

Christ was born to a young woman from humble surroundings. He entered a suffering world and enemy-occupied country, arriving not in a palace or well-equipped maternity ward. Instead, since there was "no room in the inn," he was laid in a manger. His early months were spent as a refugee in Egypt to escape the wrath of Herod the Great, who feared the coming of "the king of the Jews." Rather than turning aside from suffering, Jesus purposely went to the outcasts and underdogs. Though the religious and political leaders did not want him, the common people heard him gladly. Jesus sought out the sick and the dying and his touch brought healing. He went to the bereaved and wept at the grave of a friend. He spoke to those all others scorned, yet he knew what it was like to have one disciple doubt him, another deny him, and a third betray him. Those who once forsook all to follow him would forsake him and flee when the road got rough.

On the cross the Savior hung naked, his back beaten, his beard plucked out. A ring of thorns crowned his head, nails pierced his hands and feet, and blood and spittle poured down his side. The physical and mental agony he bore was great, but something more important was happening. Christ was *choosing* to carry on his shoulders the wrongs of the world. In those hours, even God turned away from his dearly beloved Son. Can any suffering be worse than that? Jesus totally identified himself with all forms of human suffering. Because of what Christ did for us, you can find comfort, "casting all your care upon Him, for He cares for you" (1 Peter 5:7).

Christ Deals with Sin

Christ never sinned. He never blushed with shame. He never needed to seek forgiveness. He had no open or secret faults. Those close to him said, "He was without sin." Even his enemies could find no fault in him. Yet Jesus came into the world to deal with the sin of the world. Christ identified with our suffering, but he also paid the price for our sin.

Jesus' disciple Peter said: "For Christ also suffered once for sins, the just for the unjust, that He might bring us to God . . ." (1 Peter 3:18). When Christ was on the cross, God took all the sin of all time and laid it on Jesus. He took the punishment for it, so that we might be forgiven and set free. Jesus did not come into the world for "good people"—he would never have found any! He came into the world for sinners, which includes us all. Because Christ dealt with the problem of sin by bearing it all in his own body on the cross, he offers forgiveness and the opportunity for mankind to return to God's family.

Christ Deals with Death

Christ, who never sinned, need never have died. He said, "No man can take my life from me: I have power to lay down my life and I have power to take it up again" (see John 10:19). As we have seen in the previous message, Jesus deliberately set his face toward the place of his death and became the sacrificial Lamb. Christ chose to be born, though he was born to die. And he chose to die. Willingly he went through the valley of death for us all. Christ was buried but three days later he rose from the dead. He is alive now and is able to deal with the problem of death by giving his resurrection life to us.

Claiming the Answer

To find Christ as the answer to life's greatest needs, there must be a response to his love. You, too, must claim the prize—the marvelous gift that God offers to all people. Christians are those who have come to a moment when they completely accept Christ as their personal Savior and Lord. The Bible calls this "conversion." As soon as someone is converted, Christ begins to deal with the three main problems in that person's life.

1. *Christ deals with your suffering.* Jesus never promised Christians an easy ride through life. In fact, he said, "If anyone desires to come after Me, let him deny himself, and take up his cross, and follow Me" (Matt. 16:24). To follow Christ is to swim against the world's tide. However, the Lord Jesus promises to be always with those who trust him. He is your joy—a very present help in time of trouble (Ps. 46:1). Betsie ten Boom was imprisoned and brutally treated in Ravensbruck concentration camp during World War II. Before dying there, she said to her older sister, Corrie, "If ever you get out of this place, go and tell the world that no matter how deep the pit, He is deeper still." Far from being an insurance policy against difficulties, Christianity is your guarantee of God's peace, even if you cannot explain why you are the one who is having to suffer. You cannot understand all there is to know about suffering, but you can know that it is possible through it all to experience *God's peace,* his answer to the problem of suffering.

2. *Christ deals with your sin.* God never made the world to be as it is. Sin is the basic cause of all our other problems. When you ask Christ to be your Savior and Lord, he immediately forgives all sin. All the wrong you have ever done is removed. "Says the LORD, 'Though your sins are like scarlet, they shall be as white as snow . . .'" (Isa. 1:18). A lifetime of sin can be cleansed in less than an instant. When you trust Christ, you find that your desires change. You receive a new power to be able to overcome sin. Once you may have run after sin; now you run away from it. As years of Christian living unfold, God continues his work in you to make you more as Christ would have you be. This work is completed in heaven. On earth the Christian is freed from the penalty and power of sin. In heaven the Christian is also freed from

sin's presence forever. God's answer to the problem of sin is *his pardon*.

3. *Christ deals with your death*. For the Christian, death is not a tragic end or a loss of all things. In the moment of conversion, God disposes of your past and henceforth directs your future. Eventually Christ will deliver you from death. A Christian need not fear life's end, because Christ died to deal with the sting of death, which is sin, and rose again to give his lasting presence in life, death, and eternity. Though we deserve hell, God promises heaven to all who turn from their sin and repent, trusting Christ as their personal Savior and Lord. The answer to sorrow and death is *God's presence*.

What you do with Jesus matters for all eternity. It is vital that you get right with God and start to live for him by submitting every part of your being to him. Then you will discover Christ to be the answer to your problems of suffering, sin, and death.

. . . *And this is the victory that has overcome the world—our faith* (1 John 5:4).